Silk
Pa

BM		LM	1/04
BT		LW	
CW		LX	
HC		RO	
HS		RX	
HX		WE	
KG		ZB	
LD		ZF	

Silk Painting

Jenni Milne

The Art of Crafts

First published in 1999 by
The Crowood Press Ltd
Ramsbury, Marlborough
Wiltshire SN8 2HR

British Library Cataloguing-in-Publication Data

A catalogue record for this book is available from the British Library.

ISBN 1 86126 215 9

Dedication

For Luke, Simon and Ian

Acknowledgements

I would like to thank all the amazing people I have had the joy to meet and teach over
the years, who have made the pleasure of silk painting all the greater. To Heather
Thwaites, who now has nimble fingers and an in-depth knowledge of computers, thank
you for your typing. To Chris Robbins, photographer extraordinaire, who has managed
to capture the beauty of the silk so magnificently, a huge thank you. To my family and
friends – where would I be without you?

Typeface used: Melior © Adobe Systems Inc.

Photography by Chris Robbins CPAGB. BPE2.
Designed and typeset by Annette Findlay
Printed and bound by Leo Paper Products, China

Contents

1 Introduction

Painting on silk is easy, relaxing and the results can be magical. With a few basic materials: paints, a brush, gutta, an embroidery frame and a piece of silk, you can start. All you need to do is conquer your apprehension and once you have put your first brush stroke on to the silk and watched the colour spread, you will be hooked. As we get older we sometimes forget how to play; routine jobs take over our lives and we do not indulge ourselves or find time for something new. Start silk painting with a friend – it can be an ideal way to share the cost and have fun at the same time.

There are many projects in this book for you to try, some covering a wide range of basic techniques, and some combining these techniques for those of you wishing to be more adventurous. Silk has wonderful qualities, and with such a variety available your choice is endless. For the beginner though, keep it simple, have a go and you will love silk painting.

HISTORY

The Silk Road

The Silk Road is the greatest road of the ancient world – 10,000km long, the road of Alexander, Darius, Ch'ang Ch'en, Genghis Khan, and for at least 4,000 years the main avenue of communication between the Mediterranean and China. It was christened by a nineteenth-

The Silk Road.

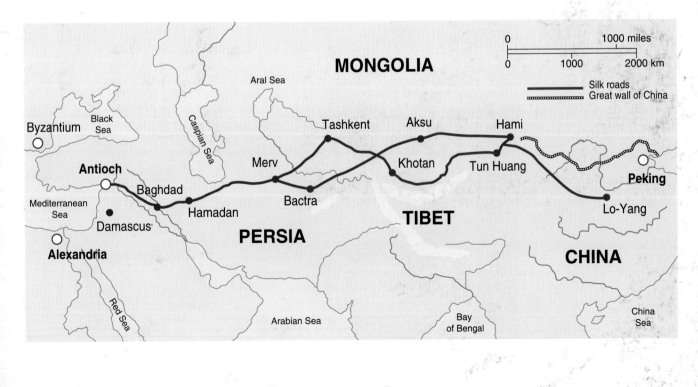

7

century explorer, but it had already been similarly named by the people of the Byzantine Empire.

For 2,000 years China kept the secret of sericulture, the cultivation of mulberries and silkworms to make cocoons, and was the West's sole provider of silk. However, the Chinese wanted rare items such as jade, lapislazuli and Asian horses from the West and so pushed their imperial borders halfway to the Mediterranean in search of them. But it was the silk that attracted the West and caused empire after empire to push eastward, some journeys taking up to eight years to complete.

It is difficult to know when sericulture began. Tradition states that in Huang Ti's time, the emperor's chief wife, revered by the Chinese into this century as Si Ling-chi, 'The Lady of the Silkworm', was walking under a mulberry tree in her garden and happened to pick up a white cocoon from the leaves. Playing with it she dropped it into her tea and found she could pull a continuous long thread from it. Certainly by midway through the second millennium BC silk cultivation was well established. Around 2697–2597BC writing was developed in China, inspired by the patterns of bird tracks in the sand. Paper was originally made in Asia from scraps of silk and plant fibres so the early silk paintings and first written communications appeared on this material.

Sericulture was so important to the Chinese that the women of every family, including empresses and princesses, were made responsible for producing silk. A prescribed proportion of every farm or garden was set aside as 'mulberry

Loom used for weaving silk.

land', where mulberry trees were nurtured and the young leaves picked and fed to the silkworms.

During several periods in Chinese history, taxes were payable in silk, so a family's fortunes often rested upon the women's skill and industry in sericulture. Skeins of silk were collected at state-controlled workshops, where they were woven into bolts of fabric, width and style being dictated by Chinese fashion and later by foreign markets.

Si Ling-chi was also credited with the invention of weaving. Chinese weavers produced some extraordinarily fine fabrics, and though sericulture spread through every household in China, the secret did not pass beyond the Great Wall for many centuries and did not reach the West until around the sixth century AD.

According to one story, sericulture security was breached in the West in about AD400 by a Chinese princess sent to marry a Khoran prince, whilst the Japanese apparently learned the secret around AD200. So although Chinese silk continued to be in demand for centuries, the quality being vastly superior, the Romans soon learned how to make silk of passable quality; China was no longer the sole source of supply.

By the middle of the seventh century AD silk had been introduced to the Mediterranean area by the Arabs. The fifteenth century saw the French silk industry flourish and held in very high regard. Indeed in later years England boasted a very fine tradition in silk weaving, but due to the levy on production and export duties England's silk became too expensive to produce and lost out to cheaper imports. The Second World War brought a boost to production when parachute silk was much needed. Now, as the new millennium approaches, the practice of sericulture is minimal. Tradition still holds occasionally, however, as English silk is produced for Royal weddings.

Silkworms

Sericulture requires great skill, knowledge, timing, patience and delicacy. Silk is produced by the silkworm, and by far the most popular species is the *Bombyx mori*, which produces the finest and whitest Chinese silk. The silkworm gorges on white mulberry leaves for over a month, eating roughly its own weight each day and shedding its skin four times before moving to the cocoon stage. Some species produce coloured silk, the hue varying with what the caterpillars eat. Silkworms are very sensitive to extremes of temperature, noise and even smell.

For several days, the silkworm produces two stranded fibres which it winds around itself in a figure-of-eight pattern. After ten to fifteen days, if undisturbed, the silkworm will burst out of the cocoon as a moth, breaking the filament as it hatches. These broken filaments have been used by many cultures to form 'wild' silk thread. The Chinese found a way of keeping the filament whole: by dropping the cocoons into boiling water they softened the sticky protein called sericin that holds the filaments together. This allowed the strands to be unwound into continuous filaments that stretched to over half a mile (800–1200 yards) in length. Several would be unwound at the same time and twisted together to make a single thread. This process, known as 'reeling', was delicate and time-consuming, the threads being thinner and weaker at the ends. If silk threads were still fragile, 'throwing' was an option. This was a process between reeling and weaving, the style and amount of twist varying with the type of silk. The thrown silk was then looped into skeins.

Cocoons and raw silk.

Today cocoons are steamed or heated using hot air, the sericin is often retained until a later stage, and the raw silk therefore has a greater strength during reeling and throwing processes. Sericin is removed by boiling or dyeing the yarn or fabric.

Waste silk, from damaged cocoons or broken filaments, was combed and spun. The resulting yarn (like wild silk) had less transparency and, more importantly for spinning, was used as insulation in winter clothes. But it was the soft lustrous silk produced by the continuous filament that attracted merchants across the world.

Early Dyes

The Phoenician dye factories, where the production of dye was held in almost as great secrecy as the Chinese held their silk manufacture, were based in Sidon and Tyre. The famed 'royal purple', so highly prized by the aristocrats of the Mediterranean world, was produced here. Dye plays an important role in the story of silk, because one of the greatest attractions is its receptiveness to dyes, particularly purple. This was so for some centuries, until the secret of manufacturing this especially high quality colour passed beyond Phoenicia, along the course of the Silk Road, and cities further afield developed the skills of fine dyeing.

Phoenician purple was made from molluscs found on the Mediterranean seashore, the murex producing the best dye. Legend told of how the god Melgarth discovered the dye when his dog bit into a shellfish and was stained around the mouth. Myth also credits Melgarth with using the stain to dye a tunic for his mistress. The purple produced was not simply the modern colour we know today, but a whole spectrum of colour ranging from deep reddish purple, the colour of congealed blood, to an inky black. The glandular liquid of the murex, a very fine shellfish, is yellow at first but is changed by the action of the sun. Dyeing could only take place in the autumn or winter when the molluscs were available, because the stain had to be collected and used immediately after the molluscs were killed. The early dye factories were therefore confined to the seashore. The extraction of the liquid was a laborious and costly process. Even today the sites of the old factories are marked by mounds of broken and discarded shells.

The colour of the dye related to the mollusc used, amount of exposure to sunlight, method of preparation and the concentration achieved by boiling. One of the rarest and most expensive shades was a flaming red (scarlet) produced by double dyeing – the fabric was dipped for a second time in a dye from a different shellfish. Such costly production made purple dye extremely expensive to use and only the richest and most powerful people could afford a whole robe of purple. Even the richest men of the Roman Empire wore only small pieces: strips, circles or squares sewn on to their white wool, cotton and linen togas or tunics. If these silk fragments were dyed purple or embroidered with gold and silver thread the cost would increase fortyfold. Purple edging on a toga marked a politician, whilst scarlet and purple stripes indicated a highly placed advisor.

TYPES OF SILK

You will occasionally come across the term 'momme'. This refers to a Chinese measurement of weight, one unit being equal to 4.306 grams per square metre. Therefore a lightweight pongée 5 is approximately 21 grams (a very fine silk), whilst a pongée 12, approximately 50 grams, is a heavier silk. A pongée 6 or 8 is ideal for the beginner.

Chiffon – a very light, transparent and delicately soft silk. Easily snagged by rough hands so needs careful handling. **Crêpe Georgette** – semi-transparent with a matt finish. Heavier and slightly thicker than chiffon.

On both chiffon and georgette, the gutta (*see* Chapter 3) does not always hold and dyes do not flow so freely. The draping qualities are lovely and they make wonderful scarves.

Crêpe de Chine – available in a variety of weights, it is a non-creasing fabric which drapes beautifully with a glorious sheen. The heavier weights are a little harder to use because the silk takes more dye. The

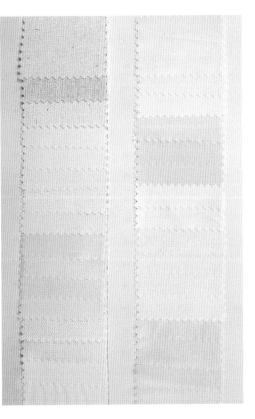

Varieties of silk.

gutta must thoroughly penetrate the silk to prevent bleeding.

Crêpe Satin – drapes beautifully, with a satin face and matt crêpe back. Can shrink by approximately 15 per cent when washed.

Silk Satin – slightly lighter in weight than crêpe satin.

Both crêpe and silk satin take a lot of dye and gutta if applied with care. The end results are worth the effort.

Habotai – sometimes referred to as pongée. This smooth silk is perfect for beginners, a medium weight being ideal. With too light a weight the dyes or paints can 'run away' too quickly and the beginner can feel out of control. With a heavier weight the dyes are harder to push around and of course it takes more dye or paint. Habotai can be used for most projects – cards, scarves, pictures and cushions – as it comes in a variety of weights, from 5 to 14 pongée.

Taffeta – a thick and slightly stiff fabric, shiny with small irregularities.

Jacquard – a woven patterned heavy silk which takes on a light and shade quality when painted. Gutta can be used to good effect but has to be applied with care to avoid bleeding.

Doupion – a tangled thread produced from a double cocoon containing male and female pupae. It is a lovely slubby silk when woven, and takes dye nicely. Gutta can be used to good effect but, as for jacquard, it has to be applied with care to avoid bleeding. Ideal for waistcoats, cushions and dresswear.

Tussore – produced from the Oak moth and ideal for dresswear.

Honan and Shantung – Named after Chinese provinces. Both are strong, coarse silks, produced from the Oak moth and ideal for dresswear and furnishings.

2 Getting Started

BASIC MATERIALS

I outlined the basic equipment in my introduction, but once you have tried silk painting you will soon be hooked and can then expand your range of materials. Below is a comprehensive list of equipment and terminology that you will find mentioned throughout this book and in other publications on silk painting.

Silk

A medium-weight habotai is ideal for beginners. As you become more confi-dent you can experiment with other types of silk to create different effects. Natural-coloured silk is preferable as coloured silk can influence the colour you are applying. In some instances this can be overcome, but natural silk is ideal. Strictly speaking, silk should be washed before painting to remove all dressing. Sometimes the dressing can be so heavy that the paints just sit on the surface rather than penetrating the silk. I have to admit I do not always wash the silk as I never manage to maintain the 'new' look, but I have been caught out once or twice. When using very fine silk take care that it is not snagged by rough hands or sharp gutta nibs.

The basic silk painting materials.

Dyes and Paints

Silk dyes (steam-fixed) are alcohol-based. They are very concentrated and can be thinned by water. The end result when fixed is excellent and the colours are more vibrant than iron-fixed paints. However, when dyes are used on a cotton and silk mix, the colour will be paler.

Silk paints (iron-fixed) are concentrated paints, thinned by water; some techniques and effects are not always as satisfactory as those achieved using steam-fixed dyes. The paints are fixed by ironing on the reverse side of the silk for two or three minutes, and as a rule this should be done before washing. Do check instructions for fixing as they can vary (*see* Chapter 9). Some silks can be immersed in cold water with white vinegar before fixing and this enables the resist (*see* p.21)to come off. If the iron sticks when pressing, the piece must be washed again to remove all the gutta.

Ironing does enhance colour. Apparently iron-fixed paints can also be steam-fixed, which improves the brilliance still further, but I have not tried this method myself. Most manufacturers advise against mixing different brand names. I have found no problems with mixing different brands as long as iron-fixed is with iron-fixed and steam-fixed with steam-fixed. But why not experiment for yourself – you can have great fun along the way.

Dyes and paints have different qualities. For the beginner, iron-fixed paints are recommended for their ease of fixing and availability from art and craft shops. However, try and get some experience of using both and compare the results for yourself.

Frames

Frames are needed to stretch the silk and keep it from touching the work surface. Start off with a round embroidery frame, as this will keep the cost down in the unlikely event you decide not to continue silk painting, and they are also very useful for testing out different techniques. Once tried I'm sure you will be hooked, however, and then you can think about larger frames. Frames are also easy to make.

Start with four pieces of wood: opposite sides should be the same length, whilst the depth should be double the width of the wood used, I suggest ½in × ¾in (1.25cm × 2cm). Many DIY shops will cut the wood to your chosen length, and all that is then needed is a metal corner bracket in each corner to stop the frame from pulling out of shape. A 36in × 36in (92cm × 92cm) frame is very useful, as you can do several projects on one screen, or perhaps a large scarf; an 18in × 18in (46cm × 46cm) screen is ideal for a cushion. There is an enormous selection of frames available, to suit all needs and pockets, from specialist suppliers of silk painting materials or good art and craft shops (*see* Suppliers).

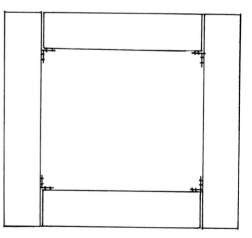

Making a frame.

Masking Tape

I always use masking tape (½in width) as it is so versatile. When using a frame stick masking tape all around the edge. The frame can easily be cleaned and no remains of paint or dye from previous work will come through to ruin a new piece. Replace the tape as necessary.

I also use masking tape rather than three-point pins to hold the silk on the frame. Masking tape needs to be half on

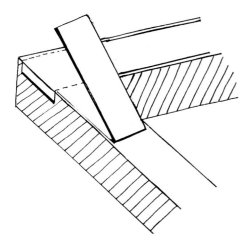

Attaching masking tape to a frame.

and half off the edge of silk. For a tight tension slightly stretch the silk width-ways and firm down the tape on to one side of the frame. For side two (opposite) repeat as for side one, and pull the silk taut. Repeat the process for sides three and four, pulling the silk really tight before rubbing the masking tape down. Silk is extremely strong so it can be stretched quite taut.

Three-Point Pins

Three-point pins can be used to attach silk to the frame. I choose not to use them as they can tear the silk whilst it is under tension if they are not inserted properly, but it is all a question of preference. When inserting pins, stagger them on opposite sides so that you do not end up with grid lines. Secure the silk with one leg of the pin and place the other two legs in the wood.

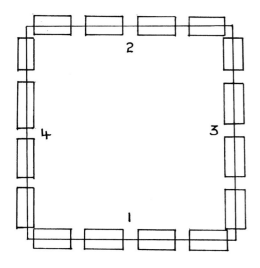

Attaching silk to the frame using masking tape.

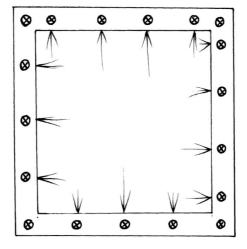

Stagger pins to avoid grid lines forming across the silk.

Stenter Pins

Stenter pins are three-pronged pins, excellent for securing silk velvet, awkward shapes and pre-rolled silk edges. They are attached to the frame with rubber bands.

Soft Pencils

3B–6B pencils or an autofade pen can be used. The softer the pencil the easier it is to rub out, especially if applied lightly. An autofade pen will fade after a few hours.

Brushes

Soft-pointed brushes, sizes 4, 6 and 8, are ideal. A size 12 brush is good for covering larger areas. Brushes with artificial bristles can be used for painting, but it is sheer luxury to use Chinese or Japanese brushes; they hold a good amount of paint and can form very fine points for intricate areas. Foam brushes are popular for covering large backgrounds as is cotton wool. Always remember to mix enough colour for your backgrounds, as it is surprising how much you need and you can never achieve exactly the same shade if you have to remix.

For wax-effect application use hog-hair brushes of varying sizes; these need to be firm and hardwearing. For more information on wax *see* Chapter 7.

Mixing Palettes

Deep palettes are handy when mixing large quantities of paint or dye for backgrounds. Alternatively, individual jam pots (the type provided at hotel breakfasts) are ideal and are now widely available.

Gutta/Outliner

These are known as 'resists' and stop the dyes or paints running into each other by creating a barrier. They are available in a variety of colours and the majority come in small 20ml tubes, ideal for the beginner. As you gain experience in silk painting it is useful and cheaper to buy larger bottles of gutta and put it into plastic bottles with a metal screw-on nib. The nibs come in a range of sizes so that the thickness of the line can be varied.

GUTTA PLUS

A clear gutta that can be mixed with steam-fixed dyes to produce coloured gutta.

GUTTA SOLVENT

Thinner for solvent-based gutta.

Anti-spread

ANTIFUSANT

Used on silk as a primer coat. When dried it prevents the spread of steam-fixed dyes, making the use of gutta as a resist unnecessary.

WATER-BASE (AQUARELLGRUND)

Used on silk as a primer coat, as above, for iron-fixed paints.

Diffusing Medium

Also known as diluant. A thinner which helps steam-fixed dyes spread evenly on silk.

Thickener/*Epaissisant*

A colourless gel which is mixed with dyes before they are applied to silk to prevent them spreading. Ideal for mono-printing.

Hairdryer

Used to speed up the drying process. It can help produce lovely techniques with steam-fixed dyes. When using a hairdryer with iron-fixed paints, however, it must be remembered that the heat is fixing the colour, therefore the paints cannot be 'worked into' afterwards as with steam-fixed dyes.

Iron

Essential for fixing colours, and pressing and removing wax in the batik technique.

Salt

A technique used to produce patterns on silk. Different salts – rock, dishwasher, coarse sea salt – all produce different patterns.

Electric Wax Pot

Thermostatically-controlled for melting wax. It must always be used with great care, noting safety precautions.

Wax Granules

These melt easily for batik and wax resist methods.

Tjanting

A special tool used in batik that has a small bowl containing hot wax for drawing.

Pressure Cooker/Steamer

Essential for fixing steam-fixed dyes.

Useful Items

A soft rubber for rubbing out pencil marks, a sponge for use in various techniques and for damping the silk, cotton buds, newspapers, kitchen roll, scissors, an old melamine cutting board, an acetate sheet, a small lino roller, rubber gloves and an apron.

COLOUR

Working with colour should be fun, but many people are intimidated by it. Relax, then think of your favourite shades and try, slowly, to mix them. Below are a few points which might be of help to you.

There are three primary colours: red, blue and yellow. As a beginner I advise you to buy a pot of each of these colours, plus a pot of black, as from these you will be able to mix all your colours. Whether you are using steam-fixed dyes or iron-fixed paints, try out a colour wheel, which is simply achieved with your four colours.

Draw a circle using gutta (it does not have to have perfect edges). Divide it into twelve sections. Position the primary colours as shown. By mixing red and yellow, blue and yellow, red and blue, you will produce orange, green and violet respectively. Position these in the relevant sections in your wheel. These

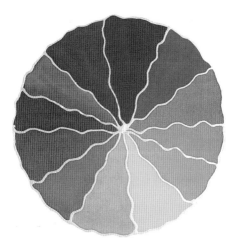

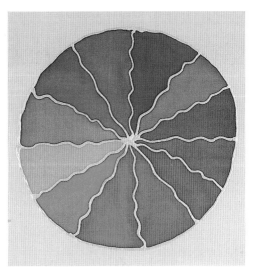

(left) Colour wheel for steam-fixed dyes.

(right) Colour wheel for iron-fixed paints.

Primary			Secondary			Tertiary
Red	(+ Yellow)	=	Orange	(+ Red)	=	Red Orange
Yellow		+	Orange	(+ Yellow)	=	Yellow Orange
Yellow	(+ Blue)	=	Green	(+ Yellow)	=	Yellow Green
Blue		+	Green	(+ Blue)	=	Blue Green
Blue	(+ Red)	=	Violet	(+ Blue)	=	Blue Violet
Red		+	Violet	(+ Red)	=	Red Violet

colours are called secondary colours. To create tertiary colours for the remaining sections of your wheel, mix equal parts of a primary colour and secondary colour.

When mixing a green, try using black and yellow instead of blue and yellow as this makes quite a different shade of green. Of course, depending on the proportion of one colour mixed with another you will get an enormous variety of shades.

(opposite) A scarf showing the colour range of iron-fixed paints.

Yellow + black = green.

Complementary Colours

Complementary colours appear opposite each other in the colour wheel. Choosing these colours can produce vibrant and exciting results, for example blues and oranges, reds and greens, yellows and violets.

When complementary colours are mixed together they produce neutral colours such as browns and greys. Red, blue and yellow, when mixed equally, produce dark grey.

Harmonious Colours

Harmonious colours appear next to each other in the colour wheel, for example red orange/orange/yellow orange.

To make iron-fixed paint colours pale, add water. I ban white when teaching workshops because once students use it they lighten all colours with white and the end result is extremely chalky. By adding water or blender (malmittel) you can achieve very subtle washes.

You will often read of alcohol being used for the same reason. Alcohol, which acts in the same way as diluant, is used with steam-fixed dyes only. To obtain neat alcohol you need a special document from Customs and Excise in order to buy it from a chemist. It took over six months for me to achieve this and was frustrating to say the least. Many students use methylated spirit, but do beware of fumes as it can bring on headaches or even asthma. Life has been made much easier now that you can buy diluant. When painting large background areas, use a mixture of diluant and water as this will enable you to paint evenly. It also allows you to match up areas before a dry edge has time to form and produce a water line.

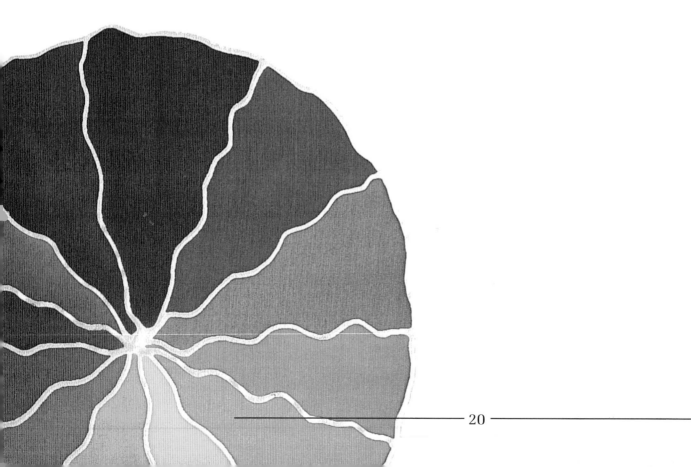

3 Gutta

Gutta is a resist that stops one colour running into another by forming a barrier. There are two types of gutta or outliner – spirit-based and water-based. Water-based outliners wash out easily in warm soapy water after fixing. The transparent gutta, or gutta plus, can be coloured by adding steam-fixed dyes. Take care not to get paints on the line of gutta, however, as it can break down, causing your colours to seep through. Spirit-based gutta is also available in a variety of colours, but when using the colourless version you will need to remove it with white spirit or by dry cleaning.

For the beginner, tubes of gutta are readily available. You might find transferring gutta from a larger bottle to a plastic bottle with nib a little wasteful, but this will depend how serious you are about your silk painting. Water-based outliners are easy to use and do not dry up too quickly. Spirit-based gutta gives very good results, but can evaporate when exposed to the air. If you find this is the case you will need a solvent thinner to mix to the gutta to return it to a honey-like thickness. Be aware of the smell of the thinner, however, as it can cause headaches.

IRIS

Iris Painting

EQUIPMENT

- silk
- frame or embroidery ring
- masking tape and silk pins
- 4B soft pencil or autofade pen
- soft rubber
- brushes (sizes 4, 6 and 8) and large brush for background
- gutta (bottle and nib, optional)
- steam-fixed dyes or iron-fixed paints
- water pot
- plate or palette to mix colours
- paper towel
- hairdryer
- iris picture or design

INSTRUCTIONS

1   Prepare your frame by covering the edges with masking tape. This will stop any colour coming through from your frame on to your work. If you are using an embroidery ring this will not be necessary, but do use the frame for painting; you do not want accidents when embarking on a piece of embroidery.

2   Attach the silk to the frame as described in Chapter 2.

3   Place the design under the silk, supporting it if necessary, and carefully trace it directly on to the silk using the soft pencil or autofade pen. Use the

Iris photograph.

Iris line drawing.

pencil as lightly as you can as it will be easier to rub out once the gutta has been applied and thoroughly dried.

4   Apply gutta over the pencil line. Hold the tube or bottle at an angle of approximately 45 degrees, press firmly on the silk, with very gentle pressure on the tube or bottle.

5   Once the gutta has been applied and the design completed, hold the frame and silk up to the light and look at

TIPS:

• When applying outliner, keep the wrist loose and every so often give it a shake to relieve the tension, because as you concentrate you tend to tense up. The idea is to produce a smooth, constant line.

• When you start using outliner a blob can form; keep your nib clear by frequently wiping the tip with paper towel. To avoid blobs, run the gutta line off a piece of paper held in your other hand straight on to the silk. This will help, but you might not be able to use this method in intricate areas. You will improve your technique with practice, so do not panic!

• When gutta is first applied to silk it stands slightly raised. As it dries out it sinks into the silk, sealing the fibres so that no paint or ink will seep through. If the silk you are using is particularly thick or slubby it may be advisable to apply gutta to both sides. This is fiddly, but it will save frustration later.

• When your gutta is not in use, push a piece of wire down the nib of the bottle to keep it free from blocking.

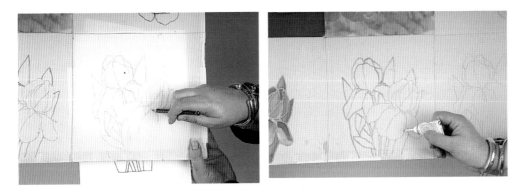

Tracing a design on to silk using pencil.

Applying gutta.

it from the reverse side. However careful you think you have been, weak areas will show up quite clearly. It may highlight lines that are too weak, too thin or, the most common error, lines that are not joined properly. All areas must be enclosed, so all lines must join; any missed or weak areas can be rectified before painting.

6   Gutta or outliner can dry naturally in approximately ½–1 hour according to the thickness of the line, or you can speed up the process by using a hairdryer. When drying a particularly thick or blobby line, do not hold the dryer too close to the silk as the gutta will tend to bubble. The intense heat will also cause a skin to form on top before the gutta underneath has dried. It is best to wave the dryer backwards and forwards, on a medium to high heat, about 6–9in away from the silk.

7   When thoroughly dry, carefully rub away any visible pencil lines using a soft rubber. Pencil will not rub out once iron-fixed paints have been applied. If you have used steam-fixed dyes, the lines can be rubbed out with care. To double check that all lines are joined and not too thin, in width or density, use a brush and clean water and fill in sections of the

design, leaving a clear area between to see if any seepage occurs. If you fill in all areas, you will not notice any that might need repair. Once this is done, dry again with the dryer, make any repairs that are necessary with gutta and dry thoroughly to finish. Care taken at this stage can save time later. But even if you have an 'accident', all is not lost.

8   You are now ready to paint. All colours are intermixable and water-based, so whether you use dyes or paints, wondrous tones and hues can be obtained. A pipette can be useful for transferring colour from pot to palette, but a brush is just as suitable for this purpose as long as you remember to clean it well between colours.

9   Lay on the colours with a dryish brush. I leave certain areas with just a brush of clean water so that the colours can very gently blend, whilst in others I put a darker shade to help highlight the shape. The same technique is applied when painting the leaves. As a rule I paint the subject first, leaving the background until last. This is because I have often changed my mind as to the colour and technique it might need. Sometimes a slightly textured effect can enhance the painting of the subject.

TIPS:

• Always work from the damp area outwards, so avoiding water lines which occur when two lines meet.

• When working in large areas make sure you mix enough colour. You will never be able to mix the same shade again should you run out.

• When you first start painting you will be content to put one colour in each area, and because you do not have to wait for the colour to dry, all areas can be painted. When you are feeling more confident, try putting water on top of your colour. This will lighten the centre of the area and push the concentrated colour to the edge, creating a different effect. Or try adding another colour to an area already painted. The colours will blend to give a natural, subtle effect. Leaves, for example, are not just green, so try adding reds, yellows or darker and lighter shades of green. There will be no need to paint the whole area as the colour will spread very freely – with just a little colour on your brush, put the tip in the middle of the area and it will spread to the edges. For the Iris project I used a range of blues.

10   I felt a plain colour was not quite enough for the background in this instance, so I used a water marbling technique. Paint the background one colour and leave for a few minutes until it loses its 'wetness'. This technique will work with both dyes and paints. With a larger brush (size 6 or 8) and using clean water, 'blob' areas of the background, leaving space between each brush mark. The water will push the colour away and it will concentrate in lines around the brush marks, creating a marbling effect. You can dry this with a hairdryer immediately whilst the lines are quite concentrated, or you can leave the colours to blend into each other for a more hazy effect. Remember: if you are using iron-fixed paints, once you have applied heat you will have fixed the colours. Marbling is a handy technique, so try it with different colours instead of just water.

Painted iris and leaves.

Water marbling technique used as background.

Large iris painting.

The iris design used here was altered from an original taken from one of the many books of designs available (*see* Chapter 10). To use this design again, play around with ideas – a picture, cushion or cards perhaps. These days photocopying makes reducing or enlarging a design much easier.

Large Iris Painting

To create a much larger piece of work try repeating your design side by side or with overlapping areas. This project, measuring 24in square, took a while to complete as I spent time getting the right balance of shapes and general proportion. It also took a while to blend and paint the colours. Silk painting is not a race and certain projects may need to build up gradually. Others, according to the technique used, may require speed and spontaneity.

Background of the large iris painting.

The background was created by working outwards from the centre of the sun (tackle this once the iris has been painted). Start off with a small circle of colour, remembering that it will spread, then gradually work to get it to the size you want. For the rest of the background, carefully paint close to the sun with a dryish brush, so the colour just butts up to the edge, then fill in the remaining area. Scatter salt on to this background – this gives just a hint of texture. We will cover salt technique in more depth in Chapter 5.

For instructions on fixing your work, refer to Chapter 9. Be careful how you store your work as it is vulnerable to marking until it has been fixed.

GUTTA VARIATIONS

To extend the use of gutta I will now combine various coloured outliners, and encourage you to mix your own colours by adding steam-fixed dyes to water-based transparent gutta or gutta plus. When fixed, the gutta will wash out leaving the colour behind. The following project involves fresh flowers, so use whatever inspires you at the time; the principle will still be the same. I could not resist these carnations as the colours were so unbelievable – an amazing vivid orange and bright bougainvillea pink.

CARNATION

Carnation Design

EQUIPMENT

- silk

- frame

- masking tape or silk pins

- 4B soft pencil or autofade pen and paper

Carnation scarf, flowers and line drawing.

- soft rubber

- coloured pencils (optional)

- brushes (sizes 4, 6 and 8) and large brush for background

- gutta in various colours

- steam-fixed dyes or iron-fixed paints

- water pot

- plate or palette to mix colours

- paper towel

- hairdryer

- carnations

INSTRUCTIONS

1   Study one of the blooms you have bought. With a carnation bloom, if you half close your eyes and study the flower, certain shapes, areas and lines become more prominent. Sketch these on to your paper from various different angles. Perhaps study the centre of the flower, how the petals join or overlap, how they emerge from the stalk. Play around with the shapes until you are happy with the design. The idea is to produce a shape that typifies the flower you are studying.

2   I produced a very stylized shape from the flower. You can easily enlarge or reduce the size of the shape by photo-copying, according to the end project you have in mind. There are many differ-ent interpretations and treatments possi-ble.

3   Cover and prepare the frame with masking tape and silk.

Sketches of carnation.

Stylized carnation design.

Applying copper gutta to the carnation design.

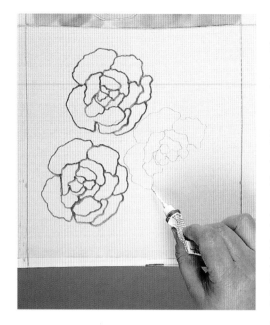

(left) Gold and silver gutta used in the same design.

(right) Iron-fixed paints used for the background contrast with the steam-fixed dyes used for the design.

4   Draw your design on to the silk with the pencil or autofade pen. You may want to use large and small shapes together, outline one shape using different colours, or use a different colour outliner for each shape – the combinations are endless. This is all part of the fun – there are no hard and fast rules, the choice is yours.

5   Apply the outliner, remembering to join all the lines; check for any breaks or weak spots. Reapply the gutta if necessary, and dry thoroughly with a hairdryer.

6   You are now ready to paint. For intricate design work, a fine-pointed brush is ideal. Take care not to paint over the gutta; the colour will spread so there is no need to paint right up to the line.

A combination of gold and silver gutta was used to outline this shape. I mixed a range of colours, but notice how, when painted next to the silver and then to the gold, the same colour varies, giving the appearance of a slightly different shade. This in itself would be a great idea for you to experiment with at a later date.

The contrast here produces a much more clipped and defined design. For even greater contrast the background was painted with iron-fixed paints and the carnation shapes with steam-fixed dyes. I am fortunate enough to be able to use both types, and if you are able to try steam-fixed dyes I would recommend it, as the colours are clear and vibrant. In

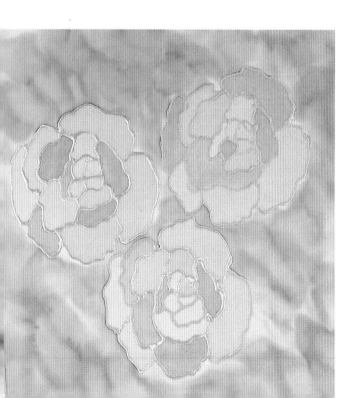

Design created using coloured gutta and iron-fixed paints.

- soft rubber

- brushes (sizes 4, 6 and 8) and large brush for background

- gold gutta

- steam-fixed dyes or iron-fixed paints

- paper towel

- hairdryer

- dishwasher salt

- carnation design

Carnation scarf.

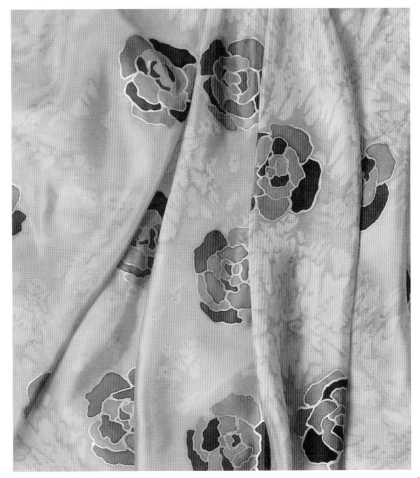

this instance you would fix the paints with an iron and then steam-fix the dyes.

A blue gutta and iron-fixed paints were used for this design. With harmonious colours you can produce a gentle effect of colour which is easier on the eye. Iron-fix paints produce a slight matt finish.

Having experimented with shape and colour, use your design to produce a scarf or cushion, for example.

Carnation Scarf

EQUIPMENT

- silk (36in square scarf, with ready-rolled edges if possible)

- frame

- masking tape or silk pins

- 4B soft pencil or autofade pen

INSTRUCTIONS

1   Cover and prepare the frame with masking tape and silk. Draw on the design with a soft pencil or autofade pen. Outline the shapes with gutta. Check thoroughly for weak areas, repair as necessary and dry with the hairdryer. For a large project such as this, check the shapes once again with clear water, just to make sure there is no seepage.

2   Now you can start painting. The beauty of silk is the sheen and, as the light catches it, it enhances whatever design has been painted. These harmonious colours work well, the yellow being on the rich, golden/orange side, running into the reds, oranges and pinks used in the carnation shapes. Because the carnation shapes are painted with flat colour, the background looks better with a texture effect.

3   Make sure you mix up enough colour to cover the large background area. It is better to mix too much than too little, and any remaining colour can be saved in a lidded pot for another project. Once the background of the scarf has been painted, scatter salt on to the wet background, taking care no salt grains fall into the previously painted areas. Leave it to dry.

4   Once it is dry, brush off the salt. Fix the work as appropriate. This design would work equally well with contrast or complementary colours – it all depends on your mood.

TRANSPARENT WATER-BASED GUTTA

There are one or two things to be aware of when you are using this outliner. First,

take care not to paint too close to the line or overwet an area. As the gutta is water-based, it will start to break down with water, and as a consequence it can lead to leaking edges. Second, if you are steam-fixing, the gutta can become tacky, so make sure the item is well wrapped prior to steaming in order that the colours and gutta do not come through the layers to spoil your work.

There is a transparent spirit-based gutta available, but this needs to be removed with white spirit or by dry cleaning. Once the colours have been fixed, the water-based gutta will simply wash out with warm soapy water.

We have now gone through several treatments of the carnation; the last one is intended to open your mind to a few suggestions of how to tackle a project. On being handed a flower, the natural reaction is to say 'I can't paint that'. We all see things in different ways – just because your view is different from a friend's, it does not mean she is right and

Carnation painting using transparent water-based gutta.

you are wrong, or vice versa. We all have our own interpretation. When you attempt it, this painting will be so much easier than you think, so take it step by step and I am sure that you will be thrilled with the results.

Carnation Painting

EQUIPMENT

- silk

- frame

- masking tape or silk pins

- 4B soft pencil or autofade pen

- soft rubber

- brushes (sizes 4, 6 and 8) and large brush for background

- transparent water-based gutta

- steam-fixed dyes or iron-fixed paints

- water pot

- plate or palette to mix colours

- paper towel

- hairdryer

- vase of fresh carnations or previous sketches

INSTRUCTIONS

1   Cover and prepare the frame with masking tape and silk.

2   Very lightly, and preferably with the soft pencil rather than the autofade pen, draw the outlines of the flowers in the vase straight on to the silk. You do not have to draw the vase unless you particularly want to. If you did some sketches for the earlier carnation projects, you will have looked closely at the flower and have an understanding of the flower head. It is not necessary to draw every minute detail, as you need only the essence or impression of the flower. The beauty of a carnation is that it rambles and curls, so a random squiggle will more than give the look you need.

3   Apply the gutta carefully, checking that all relevant lines are joined. Dry thoroughly, repair lines if necessary and dry again.

4   This painting effect was achieved by blending the colours within the petals. Apply a tiny amount of clean water to the middle of the shape to be painted. Add to this some pale colour to match the shade of the carnation and then, at the top edge of the petal and with a dryish brush, add the vibrant pink. As this dries, the various shades blend quite naturally, giving the impression of graduated colour. The colour you apply will dry very much lighter, so try to compensate by mixing stronger shades. Should you need to add more colour to the whole petal, I suggest that you carefully wet the area and strengthen the colour as necessary. If it is just to highlight or intensify the edge, use a fairly dry brush and gently add the colour to the top.

5   Approach the leaves in the same way, layering various shades and colours close to or on top of each other, according to the effect you want to achieve.

6   Make sure you mix enough colour to complete the background. Work methodically and swiftly, as if it is a

large area, as it can dry out quite quickly and you will want to avoid water lines. You could add diluant to your background, which slows down the drying process (*see* Chapter 4).

7   When you have finished painting, fix as appropriate, then wash in warm soapy water and rinse in cold water. As this is a picture, I suggest that once the silk has been dried and finally ironed, you mount it on to a white background. You will be amazed how white will 'throw up' and accentuate the colours. For larger pictures I pad the silk underneath so that the light has even more chance to catch the sheen and show off the work to better effect.

Clematis line drawing.

CLEMATIS

We all have access to an inordinate amount of resources for painting projects and can easily find something within a magazine that will inspire us. I found an old photograph of a clematis (I cannot take the credit for growing this lovely specimen!), which is an ideal starting point. As you can see, the line drawing I took from the photograph is my interpretation of the flower head, not an exact drawing.

Clematis Flower Cushion (I)

EQUIPMENT

- silk

- frame

- masking tape and silk pins

- 4B soft pencil or autofade pen

- soft rubber

- brushes (sizes 4, 6 and 8) and large brush for background

- transparent water-based gutta

- steam-fixed dyes or iron-fixed paints

- water pot

Clematis photograph.

- ◆ plate or palette to mix colours

- ◆ paper towel

- ◆ hairdryer

- ◆ resource material, for example a magazine picture or photograph

INSTRUCTIONS

1   Cover and prepare the frame with masking tape and silk.

2   Draw the design on to the silk with a soft pencil or autofade pen. For this cushion two sizes of the line drawing were used, easily achieved with a photo-copier. You will need only a few pattern repeats so that detail can be painted into each shape without the cushion becom-ing 'too busy'.

3   When painting it is important to get the colours to blend naturally, rather

Clematis cushions.

Clematis cushion and line drawing.

Close-up of clematis
cushion.

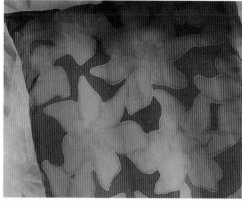

Light and shade effect created using transparent
water-based gutta.

than having straight lines of colour. For
the blended effect, put clear water into
the shape, taking care not to get it overwet, then brush a stripe of bright
bougainvillea or cyclamen down the
middle of each petal, from the flower
centre to the tip. Because the colour has
been applied to a wet area the edges of
the stripe will bleed outwards and find
their own level, leaving the concentrated
colour in the centre. Repeat this process
for each flower head.

4   Make sure you mix enough colour
to complete the background – any extra
can be used to paint a piece of silk for the
back of the cushion or saved for another
project.

5   When you have finished painting,
fix as appropriate, then wash in warm
soapy water to remove the gutta. This
will leave a white line of silk around
each flower.

6   If you are using embroidery threads
to enhance your work you can also use
any leftover paint to colour them. The
threads used to quilt around the clematis
were dyed this way, fixing the colours as
you would for silk.

7   Prior to making this up as a cushion, embellish the centres of the flowers
with various sizes of beads.

Clematis Flower Cushion (II)

EQUIPMENT

- silk

- frame

- masking tape and silk pins

- 4B soft pencil or autofade pen

- soft rubber

- brushes (sizes 4, 6 and 8) and large
  brush for background

- transparent water-based gutta

- steam-fixed dyes or iron-fixed
  paints

- water pot

- plate or palette to mix colours

◆ paper towel

◆ hairdryer

◆ clematis design

INSTRUCTIONS

1   Cover and prepare the frame with masking tape and silk.

2   Paint stripes of colour right across the silk. I have used pink/orange/pink. Let the paint dry naturally; do not use a hairdryer if you are using iron-fixed paints as this will set the colour, and for this project you will be adding more colour so the paint must remain unfixed.

3   Draw the outline of the clematis shape all over the silk and then cover the lines with transparent gutta. Let the gutta dry naturally and thoroughly.

4   When the gutta is dry, paint the original colours again over the background of the design, outside the clematis shape. You may feel you want to add even more colour to emphasize the light and dark areas. The idea is to build up a contrast between the background and the pattern.

5   When you have finished painting, fix as appropriate, then wash the silk in warm soapy water to remove the gutta. Rinse in cold water, then iron. In this design you will not be aware that gutta was used, as the original colours were painted prior to the application of the outliner.

6   Make up the cushion. This technique can be very useful to give depth to an overall design, especially as you need not restrict yourself to just one or two layers.

Stripes of colour painted on to silk.

Second coat of silk paint is used on the background around clematis shapes.

HYDRANGEA

Some silk paints will also paint on natural fibres such as cotton and cotton and silk mix (silco). For this project we are again using flowers for the basic design, however this time I have used silk flowers, which makes available all the varieties that would ordinarily be out of season.

Hydrangea Lampshade

EQUIPMENT

- plain white or cream lampshade, cotton or silk covering a heat-resistant lining

- brushes (sizes 4, 6 and 8) and large brush for background

- 4B soft pencil

- soft rubber

- silver gutta

- iron-fixed paints

- water pot

- plate or palette to mix colours

- paper towel

- hairdryer

- hydrangea design

INSTRUCTIONS

1 Carefully copy the four-petal hydrangea shape on to the lampshade, drawing very lightly with a pencil. Overlap the petals to create a pattern all round the lampshade. Add a few leaf shapes.

Silk hydrangea, line drawing and painted lampshade.

2 Carefully cover the pencil lines with silver gutta. If you take care to cover the lines totally, rubbing out after the gutta has dried will be less of a problem. The pencil will not rub out once you have painted.

3 Paint your flowers using a fairly dry brush and not too much colour. You can add to the colour gradually to build up the depth, just as you would on silk. It is also possible to add water to disperse colour and create texture if necessary. For the leaves, the same principle applies – layer various shades of green, allowing them to blend into each other to give a more natural effect.

4 The background is a little trickier to do. Make sure you mix enough colour. Using a large brush paint the colour fairly close to the design. For this background you will need to work quite quickly. Initially it will appear to go blotchy. Do not worry; as you paint round the shade the colour will even itself out as it dries. Be careful when painting close to your outline – too much wetness on your brush might seep under the gutta and bleed into your design.

5 When you have finished painting, leave the lampshade to dry naturally for a while and then dry thoroughly with the hairdryer, which will set the colour. Lampshades can be particularly effective, especially when the light is switched on, enhancing the design. You could paint your fabric on a frame first and then stick it to a piece of adhesive-backed lampshade plastic, readily available from craft shops. Another method is to follow lampshade-making instructions involving lining and wrapping the frame, producing a much more professional finish. My example is an easy and quick way to brighten up a plain shade or complement a room.

Hydrangea line drawing.

Lampshade and blue cushion; the cushion was created using transparent water-based gutta and quilting.

- soft rubber
- brushes (sizes 4, 6 and 8) and large brush for background
- silver and transparent water-based gutta
- steam-fixed dyes or iron-fixed paints
- water pot
- plate or palette to mix colours
- paper towel
- hairdryer
- hydrangea design

Hydrangea Cushions

EQUIPMENT

- silk
- frame
- masking tape and silk pins
- 4B soft pencil or autofade pen

INSTRUCTIONS

1   Cover and prepare the frame with masking tape and silk.

2   Draw your design on to the silk with a soft pencil or autofade pen. For this project the shapes were drawn with rounder edges, slightly modifying the line-drawn illustration.

(left) Blue hydrangea cushion.

(right) Apply gutta to the centre of the flowers.

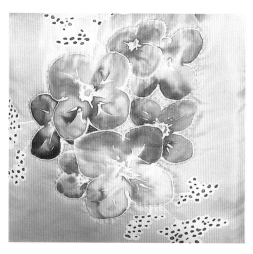

Using silver gutta.

Embellished pink cushion with machine embroidery.

3   For the blue cushion: draw over the pencil lines with the transparent gutta and check that all lines are joined. Repair where necessary and dry thoroughly with the hairdryer.

For the pink cushion: use silver gutta instead of transparent gutta, as above.

4   Apply paints or dyes on a fairly dry brush to the centre of each area and work the paint outwards. Avoid touching the outline with the brush. All combinations of colour work well for this design — whatever you choose will depend on your mood.

5   When you have finished painting, dry thoroughly and fix as appropriate. Wash the painting on which transparent gutta has been used in warm soapy water once it has been fixed, to wash out the gutta and leave a white line of silk.

6   Embellish the work by either quilting or machine embroidery. When these two cushions were made up I enclosed a muslin bag filled with pot pourri.

Hydrangea Painting (freehand)

Instead of doing a series of sketches on paper prior to drawing on to the silk, for this project we will sketch directly on to the silk with silver gutta. Gradually, through the various projects, I have tried to build up your confidence and you should now be able to miss out the 'design on paper' stage and work straight on to your silk. Your painting will have a spontaneous and crisp look.

Hydrangea painting sketched directly on to silk with gutta.

EQUIPMENT

◆ silk

◆ frame

◆ masking tape and silk pins

◆ brushes (sizes 4, 6 and 8) and large brush for background

◆ silver gutta

◆ steam-fixed dyes or iron-fixed paints

◆ water pot

◆ plate or palette to mix colours

◆ paper towel

◆ hairdryer

◆ silk hydrangea

Pink hydrangea cushion and freehand sketched painting.

INSTRUCTIONS

1   Cover and prepare the frame with the masking tape and silk.

2   Carefully study your flower for a few moments, just to clarify in your mind the shape and the way in which the petals and leaves overlap each other. Then draw directly and firmly on to the silk using the gutta tube or nibbed bottle, pressing only gently on the tube or bottle. Do not try to draw to include every minute detail. Keep your wrist relaxed to let the lines flow freely. Think of the gutta tube as a pencil and roughly sketch what you see in the flower. Your picture will have a completely different look from the carefully drawn gutta lines of the previous projects; it will have a natural lightness and freedom. Check your work to make sure the gutta lines are joined in the appropriate places, make any necessary repairs and dry thoroughly with the hairdryer.

3   Paint your design using a size 4 or 6 brush; these will enable you to get to the more intricate areas without painting over the gutta lines. Keep the painting as light and spontaneous as the drawing. For the leaves, blend several colours, bearing in mind that leaves are not just one shade of green.

4   When you have finished painting, fix as appropriate.

5   Mount your silk on to a white background; the white will highlight the colour, making it look more 'brilliant'.

6   Frame your work.

Jug with Hydrangeas (using antifusant)

I have included this project here as it continues the hydrangea theme; for other projects using this technique *see* Chapter 6. This painting is 24in square and is a free interpretation of the jug with hydrangeas. The silk has been treated with an inhibitor (antifusant) and this stops the paints or dyes from spreading. The result of the inhibitor is that it is more like painting on paper than on silk. The previous project used the gutta in a free way, this project uses the paint in the same style.

EQUIPMENT

 ◈ silk

 ◈ frame

 ◈ masking tape and silk pins

 ◈ brushes (sizes 4, 6 and 8) and large brush for background

 ◈ steam-fixed dyes or iron-fixed paints

 ◈ water pot

 ◈ plate or palette to mix colours

 ◈ paper towel

 ◈ hairdryer

 ◈ silk hydrangeas

 ◈ antifusant (or water-base)

INSTRUCTIONS

1   Cover and prepare the frame with masking tape and silk.

2   Cover your silk with antifusant. Some anti-spread you can paint straight from the pot, such as aquarellgrund, others you may need to thin a little with water before applying. Water-base is best used with iron-fixed paints, antifusant with steam-fixed dyes. When using water-base I tend to apply two coats, but this is not absolutely necessary. You can leave the silk to dry naturally or speed

Silk hydrangeas.

up the process using a hairdryer. This may give a patchy result, but it will not affect your painting.

3   With the floral display and your paints or dyes in front of you, you are now ready to paint. Do not try to paint every minute detail as the spaces are often more important to the form and shape than the painted area itself. Try to work fairly quickly, as this way you will be able to capture the essence of the flowers and leaves. Emphasize the curves of the leaves or petals to create a flowing line. You are not trying to achieve a botanical painting. Give yourself a time limit of perhaps half to three-quarters of an hour; you will be amazed at what you can achieve. If the edges of the paint go fuzzy, you may be overloading the brush. For paler shades add water to dilute the colour and with practice you will wonder why you ever wanted to use white to lighten the paint. By using water the vibrance and translucent quality of the colour is retained.

4   When you have finished painting, fix as appropriate.

5   Mount your painting over white board as this will enhance the colours still further.

6   Frame your work.

Hydrangea Scarf

One of the many qualities of silk is that it drapes beautifully, so for this project we will paint a scarf, using gutta in an even lighter way, to highlight a shape or draw around a shape after it has been painted.

EQUIPMENT

- silk (36in square scarf, with ready-rolled edges if possible)
- frame
- masking tape and silk pins
- brushes (sizes 4, 6 and 8) and large brush for background
- steam-fixed dyes or iron-fixed paints
- copper gutta
- water pot
- plate or palette to mix colours
- paper towel
- hairdryer
- silk hydrangeas

INSTRUCTIONS

1   Cover and prepare the frame with masking tape and silk.

2   As for previous projects I have drawn with the gutta directly on to the silk without any pencil lines. Draw random individual flower shapes, perhaps clusters of petals or leaves, wherever you wish on your silk. I used copper gutta as I wanted it to blend with the colours I had in mind to paint. Copper gutta is relatively new in tubes, but you can mix your own coloured gutta by adding steam-fixed colours to transparent water-based gutta or gutta plus. Keep the drawn lines light and free, as they do not necessarily have to join or be of a consistent thickness.

3   Use a large brush and be bold when painting the scarf. Mix the colours you wish to use, making sure you have sufficient. Paint spontaneously, as you drew spontaneously with the copper gutta – deep cyclamen in one area, quickly followed by orange, leaving it to blend while you tackle another area. Rather than painting the leaves just one shade of green, apply brush strokes of a variety of greens and golds all over the scarf. If an area is drying out then quickly apply other shades to blend. Speed really is the essence, so give yourself a time limit, say 15–20 minutes.

4   When you have finished painting, fix as appropriate.

We have covered several projects using gutta, following a different approach for each and showing that you can find a way to interpret whatever subject is put before you.

'Pansies' by Rita Williams very cleverly uses a black gutta for the outline, and because she then uses strong colours, the black is not overpowering. Black gutta can dominate a piece of work unless cleverly proportioned.

The pale soft pastel shades used by Pam O'Neil for her 36in square scarf are exquisite. The flowers are outlined in transparent gutta, which left a white line of silk when fixed, combined with crispy silver gutta lines which emphasize the tendrils, thus creating a beautiful balance.

Hydrangea scarf.

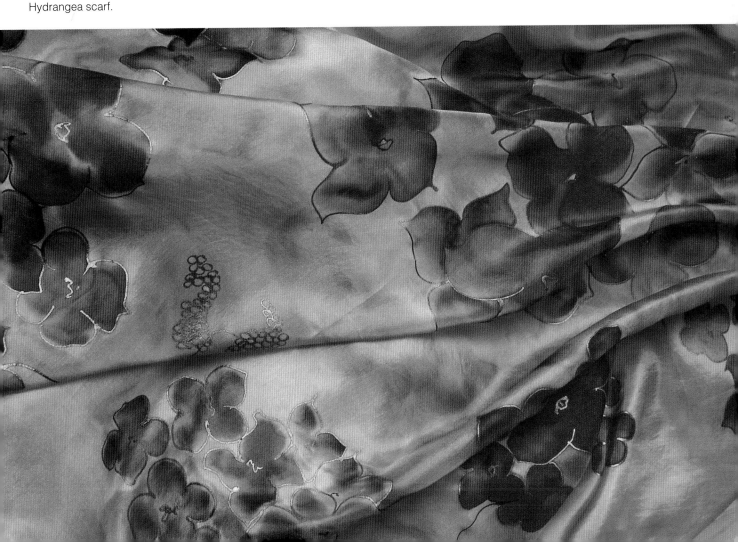

A cushion created using gutta and water marbling technique and finished with machine embroidery.

The scarves by Mary Banyard show a lightness of touch with gutta I quite envy. I find gutta difficult to use on a fine silk gauze or chiffon, and Mary proves how successful and effective it can look.

Many silk painters use the techniques we have mentioned. Nik Jory painted a glorious 36in scarf based on tulips. She painted the colours and shapes directly on to dry silk, making good use of water lines. Once dried, she highlighted the leaf and flower shapes with gutta, to enclose and form the shapes.

Pansies by Rita Williams.

A scarf by Pam O'Neil, using transparent and silver gutta to highlight very pastel shades.

(below) Scarves by Mary Banyard, using gutta on fine gauze and silk chiffon.

(Next Page) Tulip scarf by Nik Jory, using gutta as a highlighter after painting.

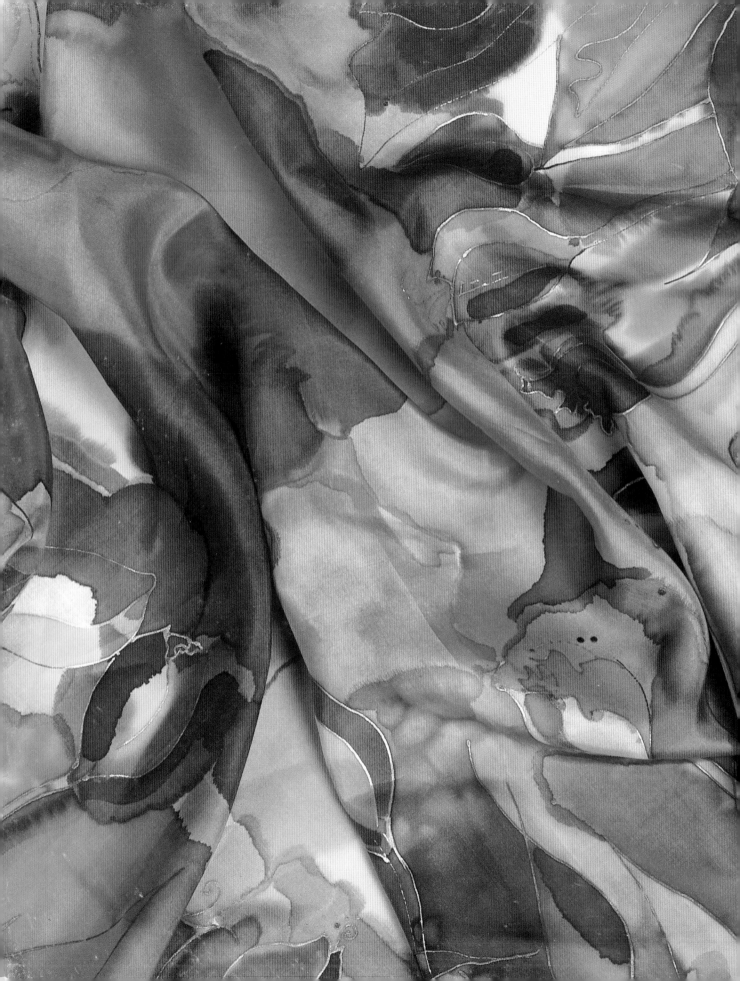

4 Water

WET-ON-DRY

Painting on wet silk differs quite dramatically from painting on dry silk. On dry silk, the paint will spread within a distance relative to the amount of wetness on the brush. When painting on wet silk the colours will not move so readily; when placed side by side they will blend together. If the silk is fairly wet it will weaken the strength of colour, so this needs to be taken into account.

A useful starting point is to experiment on a small piece of silk. An embroidery ring will give you ample room to see how the colours react.

EQUIPMENT

◆ silk

◆ embroidery frame

◆ brushes (sizes 4 and 6)

◆ steam-fixed dyes or iron-fixed paints

◆ water pot

◆ plate or palette to mix colours

◆ paper towel

◆ hairdryer

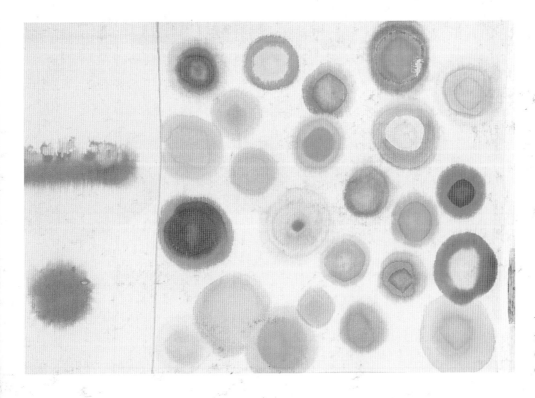

Testing the wet-on-dry technique to show how colours react with each other.

(opposite) Red sunflower, the inspiration for the scarf.

Sunflower scarf using the wet-on-dry technique.

INSTRUCTIONS

1   Put the silk in the frame, making sure it is quite taut. Using a fine brush randomly place circles of colour from the tip of the brush on to your silk, placing colours side by side, or on top of each other once the first layer has dried, or even around other circles; notice the reaction each time. Try the circles experiment with different weights and types of silk. Slub silk can produce interesting effects.

Red Sunflower

This project, a 36in scarf, will take you through the various stages of wet-on-dry technique. The design was taken from a red silk sunflower.

EQUIPMENT

- silk (36in square scarf, with ready-rolled edges if possible)

- frame

- brushes (sizes 4, 6 and 8) and large brush for background

- steam-fixed dyes or iron-fixed paints

- water pot

- plate or palette to mix colours

- paper towel

- hairdryer

- silk sunflower

INSTRUCTIONS

1   Cover and prepare the frame with masking tape and silk.

2   You might feel you need to draw a few shapes on to your silk to approximate the positions of the flowers. Draw these very lightly – if you are using steam-fixed dyes the line will rub out after painting, but if you are using iron-fixed paints the line will not rub out.

3   With a fine brush (size 4) and using dark and light brown, paint alternate colours in a small circle shape, leaving white areas in-between so that the colours can spread a little. Do not overload your brush for this style of painting as the wetness will spread too far and the idea of this project is to control the spreading as much as possible.

4   With a small amount of yellow/orange, paint small petal shapes,

The brown centres and yellow petals of the sunflower.

Add red followed by darker red to the petals.

leaving white areas within each shape. With practice you will be able to control the fine lines, but your first attempts will no doubt spread further than you would like. You must not worry about this. Painting on silk is meant to be fun, not a trial.

Adding primary yellow to the white spaces and part of the petals.

5   Next paint the red petals, and in turn their darker edge, using the same method as above.

6   To highlight the yellow/orange of the first petals, carefully paint some of the white areas and overlap the yellow/orange with bright primary yellow. As it dries you will notice shapes and water lines forming. Although these water lines will be random, they can enhance the end result of your scarf by creating 'texture'.

7   Add the stems and the leaves if you wish. If you want to accentuate the stem, paint a darker green/yellow on one side.

8   It will be difficult to paint an even colour for the background first time with this particular technique. Use a large brush, mix a pale background colour and steadily put one brush stroke next to another, being particularly careful around the flowers. If a blotchy or marbled effect

Brush strokes of background colour.

Pansy scarf using the wet-on-dry technique.

starts to emerge do not worry at this stage. Complete the background.

9   Once it is finished you may like the mottled effect, but if it is too uneven or patchy in places apply clean water brush strokes over the background. There will be sufficient dampness from the first layer to help produce a more even effect overall.

10   When you have completed the design, fix as appropriate.

WET-ON-WET

The two poppy scarves show examples of wet-on-wet techniques. Both use transparent water-based gutta, but each is a completely different style. The first depicts the paints drifting off into lighter areas and forming wispy edges; the second design allows for laying colour upon colour.

Poppy Scarf

EQUIPMENT

- silk (36in square scarf, with ready-rolled edges if possible)

- frame

- masking tape and silk pins

- brushes (sizes 4, 6 and 8) and large brush for background

- transparent water-based gutta

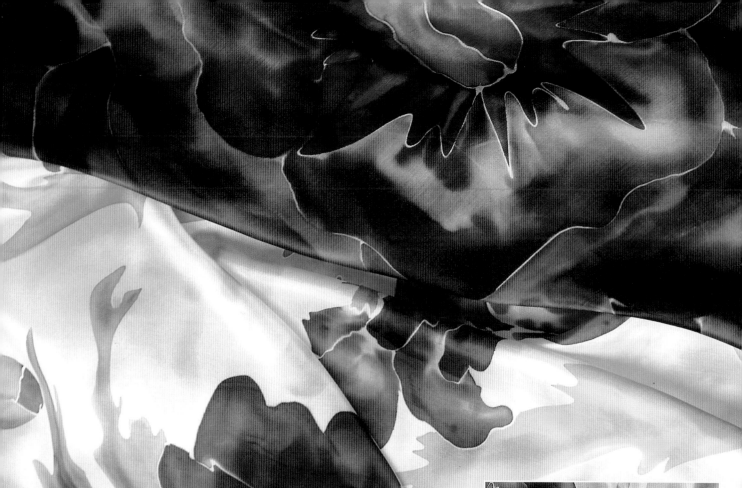

Poppy scarves using the wet-on-wet technique.

- steam-fixed dyes or iron-fixed paints

- water pot

- plate or palette for mixing colours

- paper towel

- hairdryer

- poppies (or a picture of poppies)

INSTRUCTIONS

1   Cover and prepare the frame with masking tape and silk.

2   Study your flower or picture and lightly draw an outline of the poppies, including the leaves, on to your silk using a pencil.

Poppy scarf created using transparent water-based gutta.

3   Cover some of your lines with transparent gutta. Choose the lines on the underside and sides of your flowers. The idea is to leave some of the tops of the petals free of gutta, so that when the colour has been applied the wetness of the petals gives the colour a chance to 'flare out'.

4   Dry the gutta thoroughly and check that all the lines are joined in the appropriate places. You might wish to leave certain areas free, to allow the colour to bleed, and in this case a seepage enhances the finished effect.

5   Brush clean water on to the silk, taking care not to overwet the area immediately around the gutta lines, which will start to break up if they get too damp. Whilst the area is damp, lay on your colours. As you place your brush on the wet silk you will notice how it flares in some areas yet remains fairly static in others. Do not be afraid to add a little more colour or water to achieve your desired effect.

When it comes to the greenery, poppies have the most wonderfully shaped leaves, so there is plenty of scope to layer a variety of shades of green and yellow on top of, or next to, each other. When some of the colours are left to find their own edges, the colours themselves start to separate. Some yellow greens will throw out an orange, mossy greens throw out a turquoise and blues show various shades of mauve and purple. As you become more experienced and happy to try different brands of silk paints/dyes, you will come to appreciate the quirkiness of some mixes.

6   For these poppies I preferred to leave the background with just a hint of colour, almost dirty water, because I wanted a contrast to accentuate the vibrance of the red poppies, but you may choose to colour the background.

7   Dry thoroughly, either naturally or using a hairdryer. Fix as appropriate. Once fixed, wash in warm soapy water to remove the gutta. Rinse and iron whilst damp.

Poppy-Head Scarf

This design depicts the view into the head of a large ornamental poppy, another free approach which can be used time and time again for good effect. A pansy flower would be particularly effective painted from this angle.

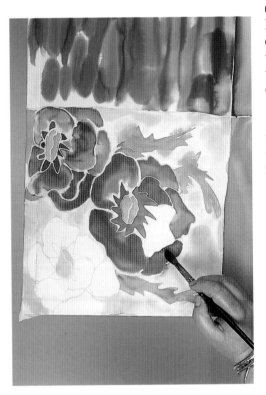

Screen showing the wet-on-wet technique.

Poppy-head scarf.

EQUIPMENT

- silk (36in square scarf, with ready-rolled edges if possible)

- frame

- masking tape and silk pins

- 4B soft pencil

- large brush

- transparent water-based gutta

- steam-fixed dyes or iron-fixed paints

- water pot

- plate or palette for mixing colours

- paper towel

- hairdryer

- poppy

INSTRUCTIONS

1   Cover and prepare the frame with masking tape and silk.

2   Using the pencil or autofade pen, lightly draw large petal shapes so that the whole of the scarf depicts the centre of the flower and its petals. This will give a dramatic effect.

3   Draw the transparent gutta over your pencil lines, checking that all lines are joined properly where appropriate. Dry thoroughly with the hairdryer.

4   Using the large brush, mix a wide range of reds and fill in your petals. A petal is not just one shade, so be adventurous – add deep cyclamen, bougainvillea, oranges and yellows. Once painted, side by side or on top of each other, they mix to make fabulous vibrant colours. If, as it dries, the colours appear to dry 'flat', highlight areas of the petals with clean water. The water will push the colour away and leave deliberate watermarks.

White daisy scarf using the wet-on-wet technique.

5   When finished, allow it to dry naturally, or use a hairdryer, taking care that the red dyes do not burn. Fix as appropriate. Once fixed, wash the scarf in warm soapy water to remove the gutta. Rinse and iron whilst damp.

with diluant prior to painting. Personally, I tend not to use it too frequently, but it is certainly worth having available. Some brands of ink suggest you add alcohol when mixing as a matter of course, so do check individual instructions.

TIP:

• Silk will only absorb a certain amount of ink or paint, so it is not advisable to layer too much. If you do overload the fabric the extra dye will just wash out, so rinse well when fixing, until the water remains clear.

DIFFUSING MEDIUM, DILUANT AND ALCOHOL

All three products are basically the same, producing similar effects. Alcohol used in silk painting is called diluant. It is readily available from good craft shops and specialist suppliers. Diffusing medium, also known as diluant, is mixed with steam-fixed dyes to help them spread more evenly. It is especially useful when tackling large backgrounds, when the recommendation is to mix the dyes with diluant instead of water. Diluant can only be used with steam-fixed dyes, it cannot be used with iron-fixed paints. Instead of mixing it with the dyes as you paint, you could cover the silk

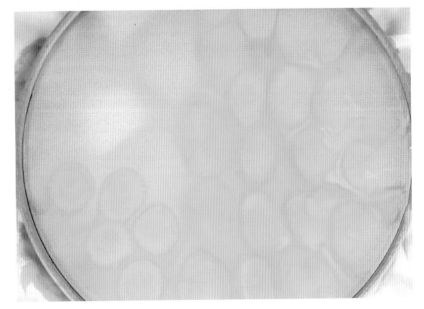

Diluant.

Effect of diluant after
painting to help spread out
and lighten the colour.

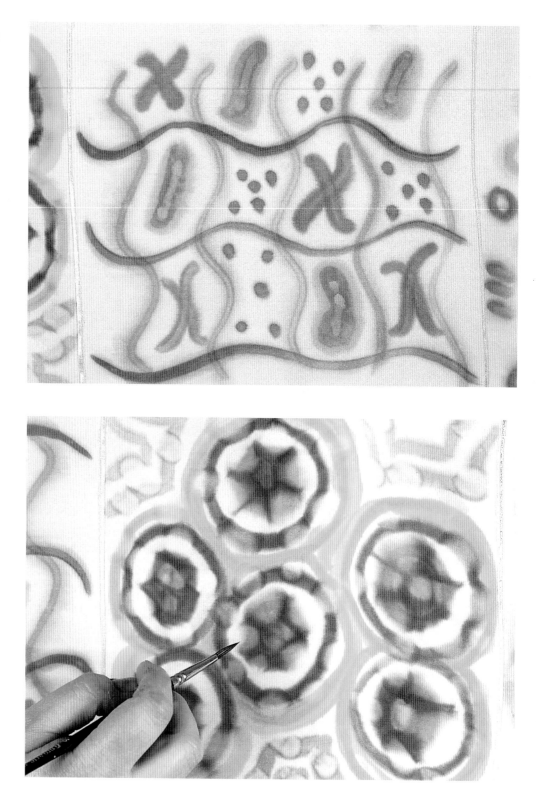

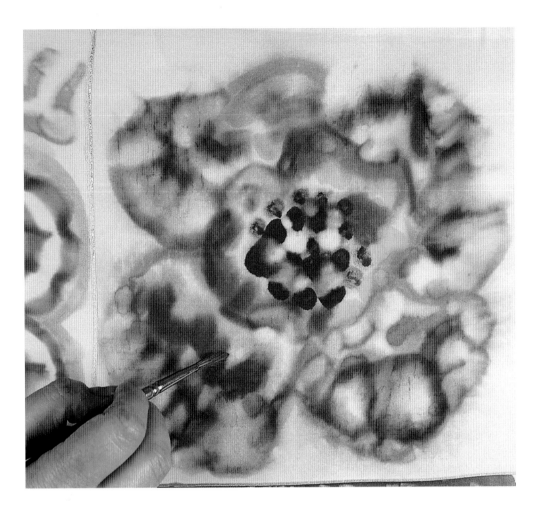

Effect of both diluant and water on the same piece of silk.

Water can be the silk painter's best friend in certain circumstances, creating wonderful watermarks which can in themselves be used to good effect, but it can also be your worst enemy. An accidental watermark can be disastrous and almost impossible to correct when on a plain painted area.

When you have finished a piece of work, put it away safely until you can fix it. Take care when putting away your things as it is easy to knock something over or flick a brush by accident. Some steam-fixed dyes need to rest for 24–48 hours prior to fixing and this makes them very vulnerable.

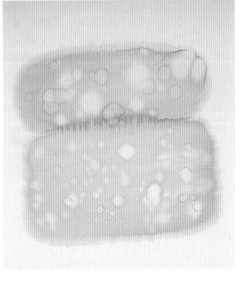

Effect of 'flicked on' water: blue – iron-fixed paints; grey – steam-fixed dyes.

Scarf created using the combined water and diluant technique.

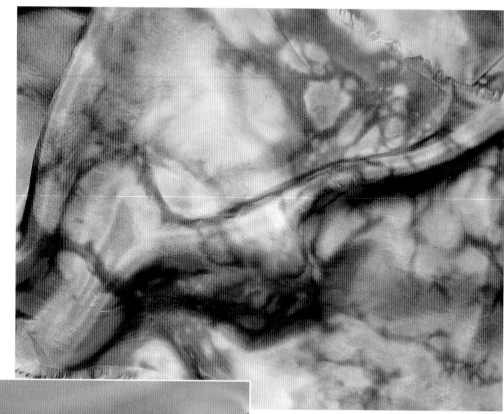

Blue paints on a wet background.

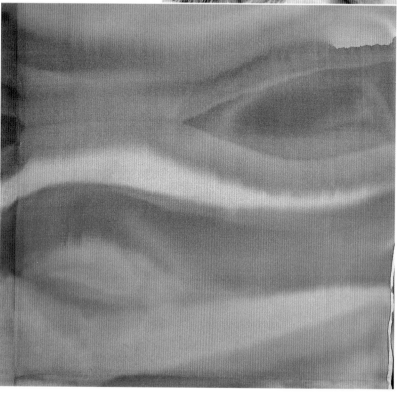

This design was created by painting a variety of blues on to a wet background, hence the colour butting up and melding together. This was done using iron-fixed paints.

This design was again achieved using iron-fixed paints, putting stripes of blues across the silk and leaving to dry slightly. It was then painted over the top with stripes of clean water. Although you can achieve more dramatic effects, this shows how the colours become lighter where the water was brushed, so pushing the concentrated colour to form strong water lines.

This design was created using steam-fixed dyes. A series of lines were randomly painted on the silk and left to dry naturally. Water was then brushed in lines, pushing the colour away, as with the paints, and also forming water lines.

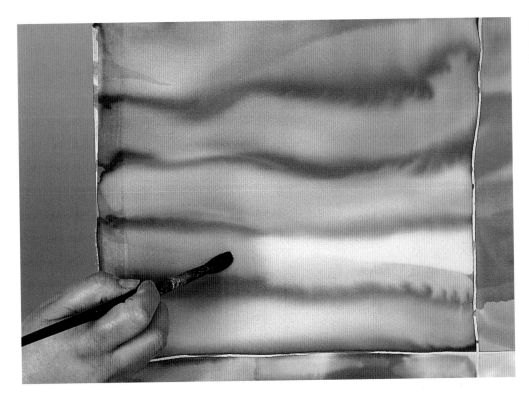

Creating random water lines using iron-fixed paints and water.

Creating random water lines using steam-fixed dyes and water.

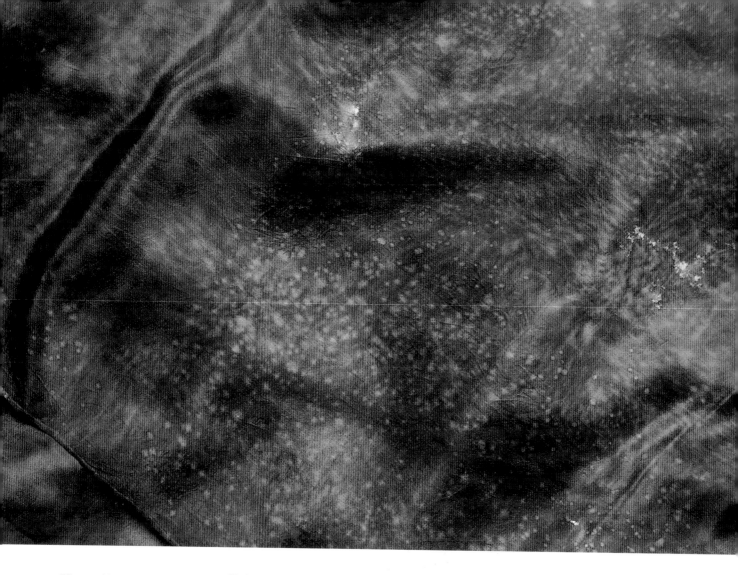

Effect achieved by spraying water through a fine nozzle.

All these techniques can be used to good advantage at any time, but they are especially effective for water subjects. Using a spray bottle or diffuser also produces an interesting texture. Colours can be sprayed directly on to the silk, or water can be sprayed once the silk has been painted. The spray leaves very fine watermarks.

5 Salt

By scattering salt on to wet silk, you can produce wondrous effects; they will, however, be random and uncontrollable. It is the easiest of all techniques and often the most dramatic, being an inspiration for flowers, trees, landscapes and fireworks – the list is endless. Different varieties of salt produce different degrees of effect, weight and slubbiness of silk, which will also alter the way in which the salt will react. The salt absorbs the damp, so when scattered on to wet silk, it soaks up the moisture, leaving patterns. It is advisable to dry the salt, either in the oven or microwave, before using it, so that it will be more absorbent. The patterns are uncontrollable, but it is worth experimenting, as sometimes using a few grains will be equally as effective as using larger quantities.

It is best to leave the salt on the silk to dry completely. In some instances it can take out most of the colour, especially if using iron-fixed paints, producing a dramatic effect. Should you wish to take the salt off whilst it is still damp, be very careful as it can drag the colour and blur the effect. Even one grain of salt in the wrong place can spoil a design and it is nearly impossible to rectify.

Keep the salt afterwards, as it can be used time and again until it is quite coloured, but do make sure that the colour already in the salt does not transfer back into the silk and spoil a design.

Four different salts widely used in silk painting: effect salt, sea salt crystals, fine table salt and dishwasher salt.

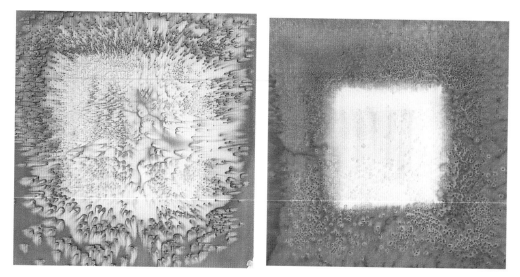

Iron-fixed paints showing salt reaction. From top left: fine table salt, coarse sea salt, dishwasher salt and effect salt.

Steam-fixed inks showing salt reaction. From top left: fine table salt, coarse sea salt, dishwasher salt and effect salt.

Multi-coloured design showing salt reaction.

Scarf created using salt technique.

A cushion with stencilled fish centre and salt technique background.

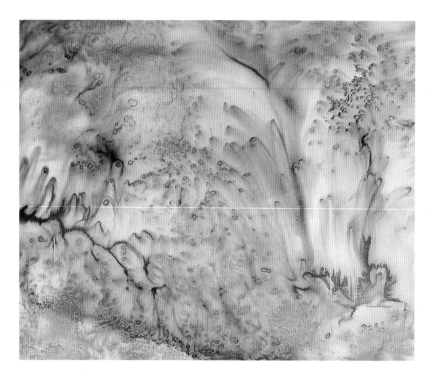

Detail of salt background of cushion.

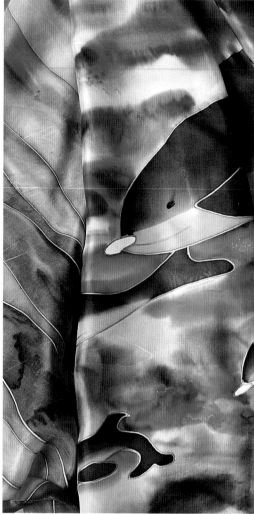

Dolphin and wavy line scarves.

Effect salt, which is produced by the manufacturers of dyes, can be expensive, however you can use it several times and it does produce dramatic effects. Dishwasher and coarse sea salt are readily available from supermarkets. They are much cheaper and produce lovely effects; these will be the two you use the most. Fine table salt, when added to a wet area, can turn into a saline solution and ruin your piece of work, so use with care. The following 'sea' projects combine some of the water techniques of the previous chapter with salt effects.

Dolphin Scarf

EQUIPMENT

- silk (36in square scarf, with ready-rolled edges if possible)

- frame

- masking tape and silk pins

- 4B soft pencil or autofade pen

- soft rubber

- brushes (sizes 4, 6 and 8) and large brush for background

- silver gutta

Dolphin line drawing.

- steam-fixed dyes or iron-fixed paints (including white if possible)

- water pot

- plate or palette for mixing colours

- paper towel

- hairdryer

- dolphin design

INSTRUCTIONS

1   Cover and prepare the frame with masking tape and silk.

2   Draw your design on to the silk using pencil or pen. You may find that drawing round the pattern you designed, rather than tracing it, is a little easier.

3   Cover your pencil or pen line with silver gutta and check all the lines have been joined correctly. Dry thoroughly and rub out the pencil lines if any are too obvious.

4   To paint the dolphins, lightly cover them with clean water and then, if you have the colour white, quickly paint along the underside of the dolphins. If you do not have white, leave the underside with clear water only. Clean the brush and then, using a dark navy, paint the top of the dolphins, slightly overlapping the white by about ¼in (5mm). If you are using water rather than white, then paint the navy to cover two-thirds from the top of the dolphins, leaving the clear underside. As the colour dries the navy will split, throwing out other shades, sometimes turquoise, sometimes mauve. The end result should show very subtle blending.

5   For the background, use a variety of different blues, some perhaps overlapping. As the colours begin to dry, apply clean water brush strokes. These will push the colours into one another to form water lines. In certain areas scatter just a few grains of salt to help create texture, but do not overdo it.

6   When you have finished painting, fix as appropriate. Once fixed, wash in warm water to remove the salt deposit. If the salt is not fully removed, the scarf will always feel damp as it will draw moisture from the atmosphere.

Wavy Line Scarf

This scarf incorporates water lines and gutta lines, which can be added after painting.

EQUIPMENT

- silk (36in square scarf, with ready-rolled edges if possible)

- frame

- masking tape and silk pins

- large brush

- silver gutta

- water pot

- plate or palette for mixing colours

- paper towel

- hairdryer

INSTRUCTIONS

1   Cover and prepare the frame with masking tape and silk.

2   Draw a few wavy gutta lines on to the silk, leaving some areas where you may wish to put more when the painting is finished. Dry the gutta with the hairdryer. Try not to tense your wrist too much when you draw on the lines and they will flow more easily.

3   Using the large brush, paint some of the enclosed areas. By using a range of colours that are close together on the colour wheel you can produce a very harmonious effect, although you may wish to add a band of complementary colour just to provide some vibrancy. By mixing a variety of shades you can over-lap some of the painted areas with more wavy lines.

4   Using a clean brush, paint wavy lines of clean water over those already painted; this pushes the colour to each side of the brush stroke, forming water lines and creating more wavy lines. You can play with this technique endlessly.

5   When you have finished painting, dry the piece thoroughly with the hairdryer. You can now add any extra

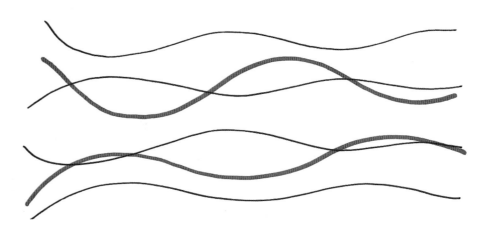

Wavy line scarf showing gutta lines added after painting.

gutta lines to highlight the wave formation.

6   When you feel the scarf is complete, dry the gutta thoroughly and fix as appropriate. Transparent gutta might be effective for some of the original lines. These lines would wash out after fixing leaving a white line of silk, so creating an illusion of depth.

Seahorse Scarf

This scarf shows just how dramatic the salt technique can be. A dark background was painted and then scattered with coarse sea salt. The salt was left until it was completely dry, which can take a few hours. A template of a seahorse was made prior to painting, but if you have a picture it can easily be enlarged using a photocopier and then traced on to the scarf.

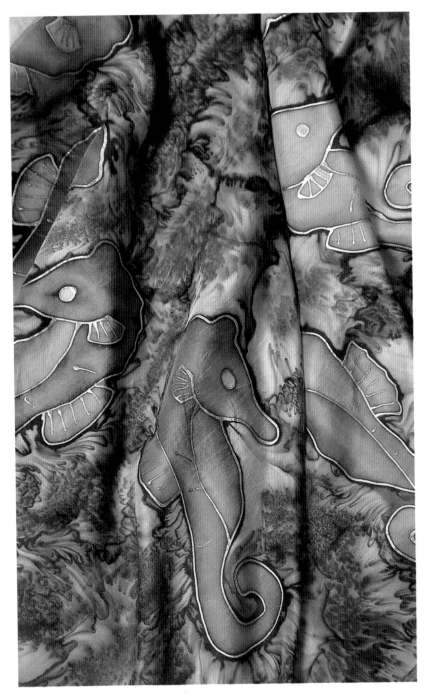

Seahorse scarf.

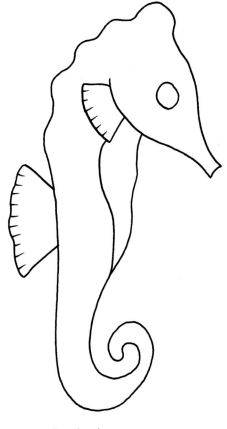

Seahorse line drawing.

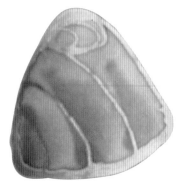

EQUIPMENT

- silk (36in square scarf, with ready-rolled edges if possible)
- frame
- masking tape and silk pins
- 4B soft pencil or autofade pen
- soft rubber
- brushes (sizes 6 and 8) and large brush for background
- steam-fixed dyes or iron-fixed paints
- coloured gutta
- coarse sea salt
- water pot
- plate or palette for mixing colours
- paper towel
- hairdryer
- seahorse picture or template

INSTRUCTIONS

1   Cover and prepare the frame with masking tape and silk.

2   Draw round your template with pencil or pen on to the silk. The shapes can be randomly positioned or arranged to form a pattern. If you are tracing your design from a picture, place it under your silk and trace the design on to the silk.

3   Cover the lines carefully with gutta. Make sure all the appropriate lines are joined. Repair any lines as necessary and dry thoroughly with the hairdryer. For a further check that your lines are joined, brush clean water into the shape. A leak will identify any break in a line.

4   Start painting the seahorses. As you will have noticed, the colours blend naturally without hard edges. Slightly wet the seahorses with clean water. Apply one of your colours with a bold stroke of the brush, clean the brush and apply a second colour next to the first; you will notice that they blend quite naturally. When you have completed all the seahorses, I would suggest that you dry them thoroughly, using a hairdryer if necessary, even if it means fixing the colours. You are about to use salt and just one grain is enough to leave a salt mark, especially if the salt grain itself is damp.

5   Paint your background quite speedily, but take care not to splash or go over the gutta lines. Scatter coarse sea salt all over the background and leave it to dry completely. Should you wish to take the salt off whilst it is still damp, be very careful. The salt can leave trails of colour which spoil the effect; the grains can also flick out to your seahorses.

6   When it is finished, fix as appropriate. Once fixed, wash the silk in warm soapy water to remove the salt residue. Rinse in water to which a few drops of vinegar have been added and iron on the reverse side.

Scallop Shell Scarf

This design is a reverse of the seahorse scarf, for we use the salt, in this case dishwasher salt, for the main design and combine it with the water marbling effect for the background.

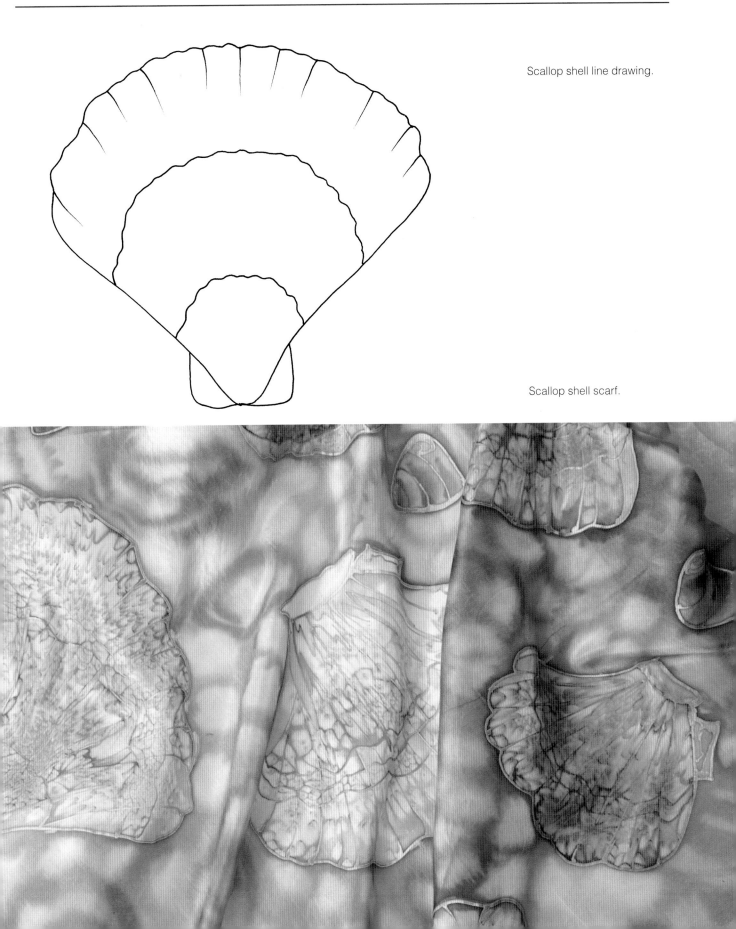

Scallop shell line drawing.

Scallop shell scarf.

EQUIPMENT

- silk (36in square scarf, with ready-rolled edges if possible)

- frame

- masking tape and silk pins

- 4B soft pencil or autofade pen

- soft rubber

- brushes (sizes 6 and 8) and large brush for background

- steam-fixed dyes or iron-fixed paints

- coloured gutta

- dishwasher salt

- water pot

- plate or palette for mixing colours

- paper towel

- hairdryer

- scallop shell template or picture

INSTRUCTIONS

1   Cover and prepare the frame with masking tape and silk.

2   Draw round your template with pencil or pen on to the silk. If you are tracing your design from a picture, place it under your silk and trace the design on to the silk.

3   Cover your lines with gutta, making sure all appropriate lines are joined. Dry thoroughly with the hairdryer.

4   This scarf is relatively quick to paint; the time taken is in mixing your colours. Brush the shells with clean water first and then add stripes of different colours or shades, side by side. You could paint directly on to the shells without putting water in the shape first; the water will just help the blending.

5   The colour must not dry out, so it may be a good idea to finish one shell at a time rather than painting them all at once. Whilst the shell is wet, scatter over the dishwasher salt. This salt gives a slightly different effect; it is more dramatic than sea salt and similar in effect to the manufacturers' product salt. Always keep your salt after it has been used as it is surprising how many times you can use it before it becomes too dark.

6   For the background, paint various subtle shades of blue and leave to dry for a few minutes. With clean water, put brush marks across the background leaving a space between each mark, so creating a water marbling effect.

7   Fix as appropriate. Once fixed, wash in warm soapy water to remove the salt residue. Rinse, then iron from the reverse side.

TIP:

• Scatter all your old coloured salt on to a scarf or experimental piece of silk which has been wetted, and the colour will transfer from the salt into the silk.

Starfish and Mussel Scarf

This scarf combines various techniques – blending colours, salt, and using gutta as a highlight.

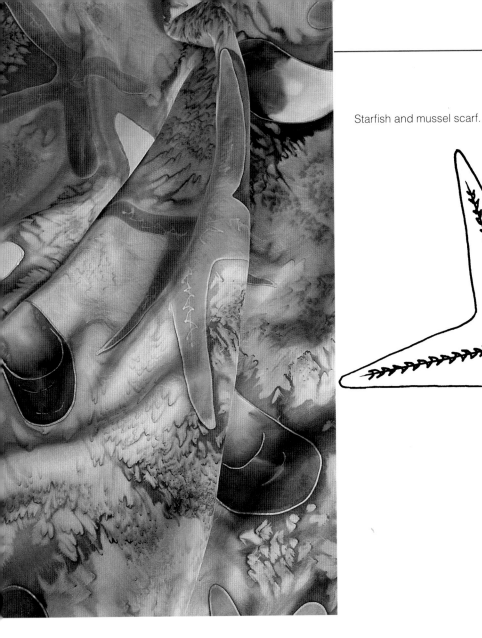

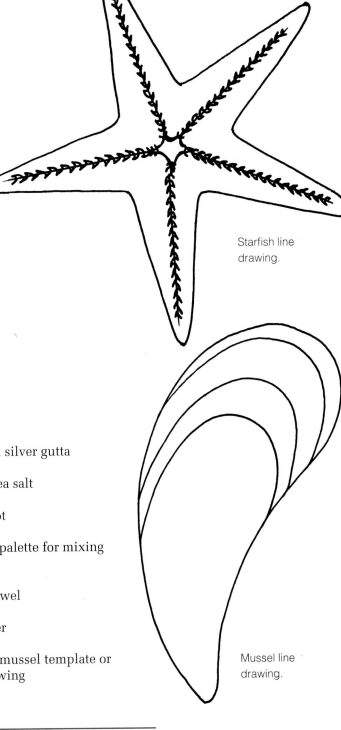

Starfish and mussel scarf.

Starfish line
drawing.

Mussel line
drawing.

EQUIPMENT

- silk (36in square scarf, with ready-rolled edges if possible)

- frame

- masking tape and silk pins

- 4B soft pencil or autofade pen

- soft rubber

- steam-fixed dyes or iron-fixed paints

- gold and silver gutta

- coarse sea salt

- water pot

- plate or palette for mixing colours

- paper towel

- hairdryer

- starfish/mussel template or line drawing

If you are fortunate enough to live by the sea you may have direct access to mussels and starfish. The pearly inside contrasting with the matt dark inky blue of the outer shell is inspirational for silk painting. I have included a line drawing of a mussel and starfish for those of you wishing to paint one of these scarves.

INSTRUCTIONS

1   Cover and prepare the frame with masking tape and silk.

2   Randomly draw the starfish and mussel shapes on to your silk, either by tracing or drawing round a template. Photocopying is the easiest way to enlarge the line drawing.

3   Cover your lines with gutta. I suggest silver for the outline of the mussels, as this links to the pearly nature of the shell inside, and gold for the starfish. My starfish was a creamy colour, so it linked quite well, but it is your scarf so you must choose your own colours. Dry the gutta thoroughly and make any necessary repairs.

4   Start with the mussels. Paint these in the same way as the dolphins on page 65. Wet the silk with clean water first and then paint the bottom section of the shell in white. If you do not have white, water will be fine. Add dark navy at the top of the shell, and where the two meet they will blend and the navy will break into mauves and possibly turquoise as it dries.

5   For the starfish, blend together various creams, oranges and lemon within the shape for a subtle effect.

6   The background is a variety of colours: turquoise, pale blues and tan.

Apply these quite quickly and then scatter on coarse sea salt, taking care that the salt does not get into any of the mussels or the starfish.

7   While the salt is drying you can add extra decoration to the mussels and starfish. The mussels will appear a little flat, so add a few curved silver gutta lines in the navy area to reflect the curve of the shell. Paint gold gutta on to the starfish using a brush, forming a crisscross pattern down the centre of each arm. Clean the brush thoroughly as the gutta can spoil the hairs.

8   Once the scarf is finished, remove the salt with care and fix the colours as appropriate. Once fixed, wash in warm soapy water to remove the salt residue. Rinse it in water to which a few drops of vinegar have been added and iron from the reverse side.

SATURATED SALT SOLUTION

This technique produces a fine dotted effect with a texture that can vary according to the salt used to make the solution. The best results are achieved with iron-fixed paints rather than dyes, and with sea salt rather than table salt. Dissolve one tablespoon of sea salt to 3Hfl oz (100ml) of hot water and stir until the salt has dissolved completely. Either soak your silk in the solution, or preferably paint the solution on to your silk when attached to the frame. Leave it to dry naturally. I find an extra coating of the solution can produce an even better effect, but this is not essential and can disturb the already formed crystals.

Geometric pattern using
iron-fixed paints with a
saturated salt solution on
silk.

Sunflower painted on
saturated salt solution with
steam-fix dyes.

Detail of sunflowers.

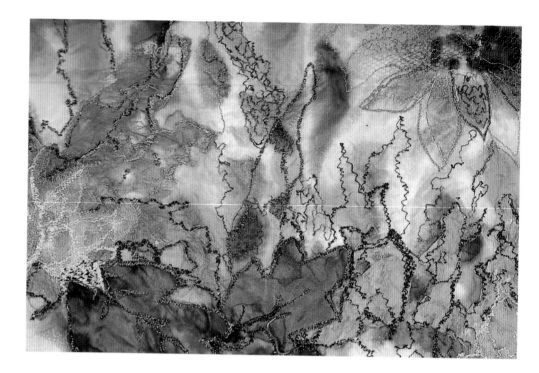

EQUIPMENT

- silk

- frame or embroidery ring

- masking tape and silk pins

- rock/sea salt solution (1tbsp dissolved in 3Hfl oz water)

- brushes (sizes 4, 6 and 8)

- steam-fixed dyes or iron-fixed paints

- water pot

- plate or palette for mixing colours

- paper towel

INSTRUCTIONS

1   Cover and prepare the frame with masking tape and silk, or put the silk into the embroidery frame, making sure it is quite taut.

2   Apply the salt solution and leave it to dry naturally in a warm atmosphere. If you wish, apply a second coat.

3   Paint on the design of your choice.

4   I would suggest that once painted and dried, fix as appropriate, wash in soapy water and rinse.

You may be able to see tiny dots at the edges of the sunflowers and leaves. This is typical of the effect. This technique can be used with most designs, and you could go on to add machine embroidery.

6 Anti-spread

Anti-spread is a clear or milky liquid that prevents dyes from spreading when brushed on to silk prior to painting. We briefly touched on this when tackling the Jug with Hydrangeas project in Chapter 3. Antifusant is needed when you use steam-fixed dyes, whilst for iron-fixed paints you should use water-base (aquarellgrund). You can also make your own by mixing one part transparent solvent-based gutta to six parts solvent (thinner).

Once the inhibitor has been painted on to the silk it becomes more like painting on paper than on silk. The silk itself will also feel papery and look transparent. Once a painting has been finished

Poppies painted on silk which was first treated with antifusant.

Poppy photograph.

and fixed you can wash the silk, but only some of the inhibitor will come out, not all of it. I would recommend this technique for framed paintings or hangings rather than scarves. A large range of techniques are possible if an inhibitor is used, such as stencilling, sponging, drawing and block printing.

Landscape Painting

EQUIPMENT

- silk
- frame or embroidery ring
- masking tape and silk pins
- old brush, water-base/antifusant
- brushes (sizes 4, 6 and 8) and large brush for background
- steam-fixed dyes or iron-fixed paints
- water pot
- plate or palette for mixing colours
- paper towel
- hairdryer
- design

INSTRUCTIONS

1   Cover and prepare the frame with masking tape and silk. You could use a large piece of silk and carry out different samples, or alternatively try individual samples in an embroidery ring.

2   If you are using iron-fixed paints then brush water-base (aquarellgrund),

a white liquid, on to your silk. Water-base does not give a total block, so a second application may be necessary. If you are using steam-fixed dyes, apply antifusant. This is a clear liquid that may need thinning with just a little water. Antifusant is certainly more effective for crisp finished lines. You can let it dry naturally or use a hairdryer to speed up the process.

A combination of techniques – colour was brushed and sponged over silk, one colour overlapping another.

Landscape.

3 Although the inhibitor stops the colour spreading, we need to blend the colours for the sky so that it will look natural. Apply clean water to this area and blend in blues and grey. As they dry the colours will merge to give a more natural effect.

4 Apply lines of various shades of green to give a landscape impression.

5 Paint the tree in a dark brown/black over the top of the landscape. When it is dry, sponge on green clusters to depict leaves; it is worth spending extra money to get an artist's sponge, as it does give finer effects. To emphasize the trunk and perhaps one or two branches, use a waterproof pen with a fine point to highlight some of the edges. You could also use black gutta for this, if you can get a fine line.

Summer view.

6 The bushes were created using a variation of a technique we tackled earlier. With the point of a brush apply small dots of green and yellow to the silk. When these are dry, apply small spots of water, overlapping the green and yellow areas. It will not spread quite as normal, but will still produce an interesting finish. Once you have finished painting, fix as appropriate. Mount your work over a white board, which will highlight the colours and make them appear more 'brilliant'.

Summer view.

Winter scene showing the reaction of wide variety of inks and paints.

Try this winter scene. If you are not washing this piece, then take the opportunity to try lots of techniques and different materials. Combine water, paints, dyes and white paint and you will be surprised how they react together. Some will push colours away, others will merge. I suggest you make notes of which has what effect, as you may want to use that particular effect in another project and you will be so frustrated if you cannot remember which paints reacted with which dyes!

For the autumn sky I suggest wetting the already inhibited silk. This technique was also used for the Lilies and Himalayan Poppy projects opposite, but this time the whole area of silk was flooded. Antifusant was applied to the surface and dried thoroughly. Water was then applied and the silk left quite wet. Into this dyes were dropped, which then shot off at all angles like an explosion.

Once the dyes had spread and the edges had begun to flare, the paintings were dried with the hairdryer. With the inhibitor you are able to apply one colour on top of another, so white highlight and stamens were painted in the pink flowers once they were dry. In theory salt should have no effect as it has nothing to pull across because of the inhibitor. With the Himalayan poppy, however, salt was scattered at the base of the picture and when it was dried it left crystal-shaped areas.

Once you have been painting for a while you will become more experimental. When you know the basics you can 'play' with greater confidence.

Experiment with liquid acrylic dyes, both matt and pearlized. They can add another dimension to your painting, but they must be used sparingly. Liquid acrylics will not bleed and will make the silk feel papery, whether or not the inhibitor has been used.

Autumn scene – sponging technique on antifusant.

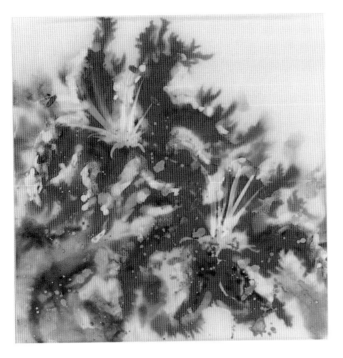

Lilies – treated silk was soaked with water then flooded with inks.

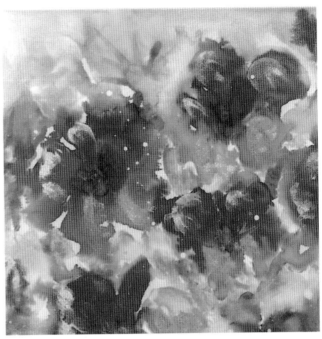

Pelargoniums – a mixture of dyes and paints on treated silk.

Himalayan poppy – treated silk was flooded with water then dyes and a little salt were added.

Delphiniums, incorporating liquid acrylics.

Poppy cushion with machine embroidery.

STAMPING

Stamping has become very popular and there is no reason why stamps or blocks cannot be used on silk. The larger, less intricate stamps are ideal. A block with a handle gives a more even pressure over the silk, and you can easily make your own by cutting into very firm sponge. A block with a vine design was used here.

EQUIPMENT

◆ silk

◆ frame

◆ masking tape and silk pins

◆ inhibitor, water-base/antifusant

◆ brushes (sizes 6 and 8)

◆ waterproof fine-point pen

◆ steam-fixed dyes or iron-fixed paints

◆ water pot

◆ plate or palette for mixing colours

◆ paper towel

◆ hairdryer

◆ block design

◆ ruler

Stamping with a block on to treated silk.

INSTRUCTIONS

1 Cover and prepare the frame with masking tape and silk.

2 Apply the inhibitor evenly over the silk. Dry naturally or use the hairdryer to speed up the process.

3 Mix your colours. The easiest method of stamping is to paint your colour on to the block with a brush and then stamp firmly on to the silk. If you leave the block on too long you get a blurred design, but do not worry. You can either paint one colour at a time or a selection of colours into your block. Gradually build up your design with several applications at different angles. It may look uneven at this stage, but again do not worry. Dry with the hairdryer.

4 To accentuate the shapes, draw randomly around some of the leaves with the waterproof pen. You could also use black gutta, but a fine line is needed to highlight the design and gutta may be just a little too thick.

Using a waterproof pen to draw trellis and highlight leaf shapes.

5 For the background, use a ruler and pen to partly draw trellis behind the leaves. There will be no need to draw solid continuous lines for this.

6 Add just a hint of blue in the corners of the trellis.

7 When you have finished painting, dry thoroughly and fix as appropriate.

STENCILLING

Stencilling produces a similar effect to stamping. There are many stencils available with which to try this technique, but making your own produces a totally personal, unique piece of work.

Violet Stencil

EQUIPMENT

- silk

- frame

- masking tape and silk pins

- inhibitor, water-base/antifusant

- brushes (sizes 4 and 6)

- waterproof fine point pen

- steam-fixed dyes or iron-fixed paints

- water pot

- plate or palette for mixing colours

- sponge

- paper towel

⬥ hairdryer

⬥ stencil design

INSTRUCTIONS

1   Cover and prepare the frame with masking tape and silk.

2   Apply the inhibitor evenly over the silk.

3   Place your stencil on the silk and carefully sponge the colours into the shape, working from the outside of the shape inwards, and taking care not to get colour under the stencil as this will cause smudging.

4   Highlight areas with the waterproof pen when the silk is dry.

5   Fix the work as appropriate.

Stencilling can be combined with many other techniques.

Violet stencil.

Sweet Pea Stencil

A small remnant of silk is ideal for this project. Stencilling will produce a lovely effect, especially when highlighted with hand-dyed threads and machine embroidery.

EQUIPMENT

⬥ silk (remnant)

⬥ embroidery frame

⬥ inhibitor, water-base

⬥ iron-fixed paints

⬥ sponge

⬥ water pot

⬥ plate or palette for mixing colours

⬥ paper towel

⬥ hairdryer

⬥ 18in piece of cream silk, such as douppion or shantung

⬥ machine and embroidery threads

INSTRUCTIONS

1   Put the silk in the embroidery frame and make sure it is taut. Paint on the inhibitor and allow it to dry naturally.

2   Place the stencil on top of the silk and carefully sponge on the colour. Sponge from the outside of the stencil inwards to prevent the colours seeping underneath. Overlap the colours with the sponge to achieve a subtle blend and create a more interesting look to the piece.

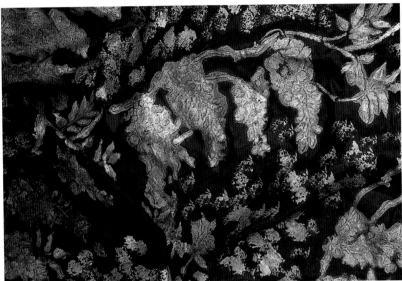

Sweet pea stencil.

3   Fix the paints using an iron (*see* Chapter 9).

4   Wash in warm soapy water to remove some of the inhibitor. It will not all wash out, but it will soften a little.

Sweet peas with machine embroidery for the centre of a cushion.

5   Lay the stencilled silk in the centre of the larger piece of cream silk. Machine- or hand-embroider parts of the flowers and stems to anchor the silks together. Machine-stitch around the edge of the sweet pea piece of silk to attach it firmly to the backing. This was not done first to avoid the silk rucking up in the wrong places.

6   Make up as a cushion.

THICKENER

Thickener or *épaississant* is a water-based colourless gel which, when mixed with dyes, can be used for printing and painting. When dyes are mixed with thickener, they do not run or bleed, so gutta and anti-spread are unnecessary. It is ideal for producing fine detail when painting on silks of varying weights, however it is always advisable to experiment on a small piece of silk before attempting a larger project. The thickener is easy to use: just add dye to the gel and stir well.

A 36in square scarf with gold wisteria stencil, using liquid acrylic inks oversponged with gold gutta.

Materials for monoprinting.

Thickener can be used for many techniques, such as monoprinting. This is easy to achieve and produces unique prints. Monoprinting can be successfully carried out on calico, although I would advise mixing iron-fixed paints with the thickener as this would make fixing easier.

A monoprint.

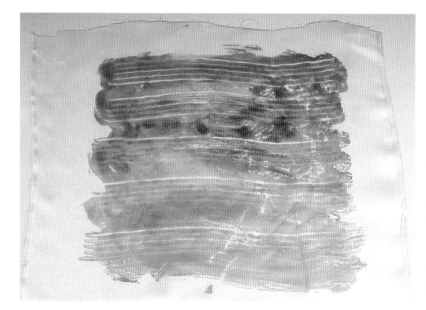

EQUIPMENT

- selection of silks
- steam-fixed dyes and iron-fixed paints
- melamine board or sheet of acetate
- thickener
- roller
- selection of brushes
- items for making patterns, for example stipple brush, comb

INSTRUCTIONS

1   Mix your colour with the thickener and put a small amount on your acetate sheet or board.

2   Create a pattern in the mix, for example draw a comb across it or use fingermarks.

3   Gently lay your piece of silk over the design and press down carefully. Peel off the silk once it is printed and leave it to dry. Although this is called monoprinting you can sometimes get a second print, but it will be a lighter version of the first.

4   Once it is dry, fix as appropriate. Wash it in warm soapy water, then rinse and iron the piece.

TIPS:

• Work quite quickly when monoprinting as the gel can dry out rapidly, especially if it is only a thin layer.

• Use a piece of acetate sheet instead of glass or board; not only is it much safer, but it can be rolled and kept with your painting materials without being bulky.

A leaf print.

Leaves make lovely prints, either by painting the gel on to the leaf and then laying the leaf on the silk, or by laying leaves into the gel on the acetate sheet and then printing.

Use thickener with the sponging technique to produce a mottled effect, perhaps laying one colour with another. Brush patterns can also be very interesting, and monoprinting is ideal for experimenting with the various shapes and patterns formed by different types of brushes. For fine detail, thickener can be just perfect.

7 Batik Wax

Batik is the process of applying molten wax to fabric, traditionally a long and intricate method of applying both wax and dyes to gradually build up designs. For true batik the fabric is waxed, then dipped into the lightest of the colour dyes, dried and the wax removed. The wax is then painted on again to allow another part of the design to be dipped, and so on until the design is complete. It is a complicated, time-consuming technique, which has to allow for the mixing of colours as the redipping process proceeds.

With silk paints the process can be speeded up, yet it will still enable you to produce lovely batiks. Because the dyes are painted directly on to the fabric, rather than by dipping, very subtle colour changes can occur in small, highlighted areas. The distinctive crackle effect of batik, usually random dark lines, can be achieved easily, but it is not always necessary.

A fox batik by Lizzie Perkins using the traditional method to dye each shade.

Stars and swirls fabric with the typical batik crackle effect.

The equipment is quite basic. Some items can make life easier, but they are not essential. A thermostatically controlled wax pot is a luxury for many people, but it will depend on your circumstances and how often you wish to do batik. I can recommend a simpler approach, but with both pieces of equipment you must take great care where heated wax is concerned – if it heats to over 60°C it starts smoking and can be very dangerous. *Never* leave any wax pot unsupervised. I use an empty steam pudding pot which fits securely into the top of a nightlight holder, always making sure the holder itself is stable. The wax

Materials for batik.

pellets go in the pot so the nightlight melts the wax as it burns. It keeps it at an ideal temperature, sufficient for painting, but do keep an eye on the amount of wax in the pot. As it gets too low it can start to smoke, so beware. This equipment can be safely used outside.

A tjanting can also be extremely useful. It is a metal-spouted hand-held tool that has a small reservoir bowl for the wax. It can aid drawing and produce lovely lines.

Batik wax is available in pellet form from good craft shops, but you can buy paraffin wax in blocks or beads. This is quite cheap and it is excellent for the cracking technique. Beeswax can be added, but as beeswax is soft the cracking effect might not be successful, although the mix is ideal for fine detail work. Do not use your best sable brushes as they will be ruined; bristle brushes are ideal. A variety of bristle shapes are available and you can always cut a brush to your own shape for a special effect. Household brushes are also fine to use.

For a trial experiment with the basic techniques, try the following example. It will highlight problems which you can then practise before embarking on a larger project.

EQUIPMENT

- silk
- frame
- masking tape and silk pins
- wax pellets
- wax pot (pudding tin and night-light holder)
- nightlights and matches
- brushes for wax
- water pot
- iron-fixed paints and brushes
- paper towel
- newspaper
- iron

INSTRUCTIONS

1   Cover and prepare the frame with masking tape and silk.

2   Light the nightlight and add the pellets to the pudding tin. While the wax is melting, work out a design and mix your colours.

3   Practise drawing with the tjanting on a piece of newspaper. Apply the wax to the silk. The wax has to penetrate the silk, so for successful application the wax has to be quite hot. When it is applied to the silk it must be transparent; should it be 'white' it is not hot enough and will not penetrate right through the silk. For thicker weight silks it might be necessary to wax both sides.

4   Apply the colour all over the surface.

5   When the colour has dried, unpin the silk, place it between layers of newspaper and iron. The heat will melt the wax which will be absorbed by the paper. Repeat, changing the newspaper when it is saturated with wax, until it has all been absorbed and the silk is clear.

6   Repin the silk to the frame and reapply wax in different areas, overlapping some of the white areas.

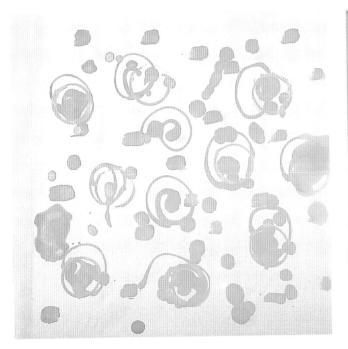

Stage one of batik – the first application of wax.

Painting the second stage and adding more wax.

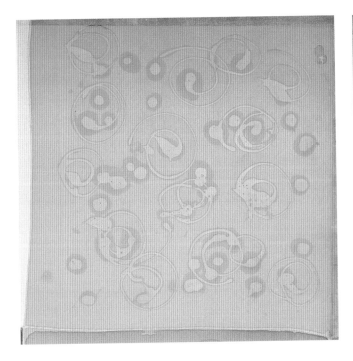

Painting the first stage and adding more wax.

Painting the fourth stage begins to reveal different shades of colour.

7   Apply another colour all over the silk and leave to dry. Once again unpin the silk and remove the wax as before.

8   Repin the silk and apply more wax. Add yet another colour and leave it to dry.

9   Unpin the silk and remove the wax completely (*see* Chapter 9). By following this process you will be able to see the various stages reflected in your sample, which will be excellent to keep by you when tackling a larger project.

Sunflower Design

This is a step on from the previous experiment and will help build your confidence for an even more ambitious project to come.

EQUIPMENT

- silk
- frame
- masking tape and silk pins
- wax pellets
- wax pot (pudding tin and night-light holder)
- nightlights and matches
- brushes for wax
- water pot
- iron-fixed paints and brushes
- paper towel
- newspaper
- iron

INSTRUCTIONS

1   Cover and prepare the frame with masking tape and silk.

2   Apply the wax with either a brush, tjanting or both and outline the sunflower. This is a freehand impression, not a precise drawing. The technique dictates speed, as the wax must stay hot to penetrate the silk. Put random brush strokes in the background, but do not overdo it as the background will be built up by the various stages of the technique.

3   Paint as you would a design for silk painting, mixing the colours within various shapes. This is where the batik becomes much easier when using paints rather than the traditional method.

4   When the paint is dry apply more wax, overlapping areas already painted.

5   Paint again. Repeat the waxing and painting until you are happy with your design. Leave it to dry.

6   Unpin the silk and remove the wax thoroughly. Finish as appropriate.

Sunflower showing the first application of wax and paint.

Further application of wax.

Sunflower Scarf

This is a more challenging project, but follows on well from the sunflower in the previous project. It is tackled in exactly the same way but on a larger scale, as the scarf is 36in square. It is an expressive technique, so you can really let go and have fun. The only messy part is removing the wax, but the end result is worth the effort.

WAX BRUSH STROKES

Wax is equally effective used for patterning alone. This scarf was produced very quickly using iron-fixed paints.

EQUIPMENT

- silk (36-in square scarf, with ready-rolled edges if possible)

- frame

- masking tape and silk pins

- wax pellets

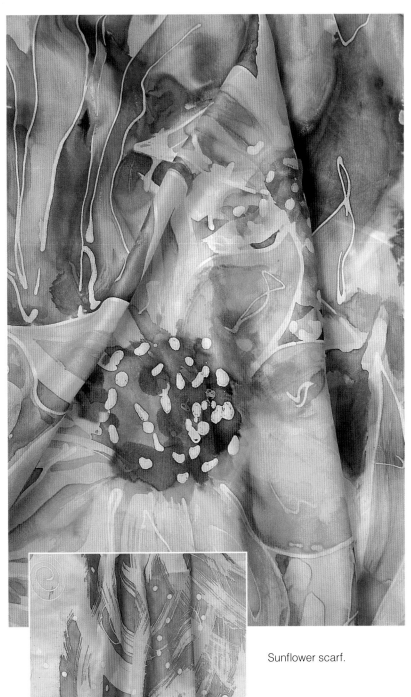

Sunflower scarf.

A scarf created using wax brush strokes.

- wax pot (pudding tin and night-light holder)

- nightlights and matches

- brushes for wax and 2–3in household brush

- water pot

- iron-fixed paints and brushes

- paper towel

- newspaper

- iron

INSTRUCTIONS

1   Cover and prepare the frame with masking tape and silk.

2   Apply the wax in small swirls and random drops.

3   Paint the whole scarf with pale turquoise and bright yellow patches. Where the colour overlaps a green will form. Leave it to dry naturally.

4   Apply the wax with the household painting brush, using a sweeping motion, leaving wispy brush strokes.

5   Paint the whole scarf with a darker blue. Leave it to dry.

6   Unpin the scarf and remove the wax. You will need plenty of newspaper to remove the wax thoroughly.

7   Finish the scarf as appropriate.

FALSE BATIK

This is a slight misnomer, as the whole of this chapter's interpretation of batik is false batik, in as much as it is not the traditional method. The traditional finish to batik is an all-over crackle effect. It is easily obtained by covering the whole area with wax, scrunching it and then painting with a dark colour. The dark paint highlights the cracks and so penetrates the fabric, leaving the crackle effect.

Puffins

EQUIPMENT

- silk

- frame

- masking tape and silk pins

- wax pellets

- wax pot (pudding tin and night-light holder)

- nightlights and matches

- brushes for wax

- water pot

- iron-fixed paints and brushes

- paper towel

- newspaper

- iron

- puffin design

Applying wax on to a ready-painted silk picture – the first stage of false batik.

Dark paint is applied over scrunched wax puffins to produce dark crackled lines.

INSTRUCTIONS

1   Paint your design in the normal way using gutta and paints.

2   Cover the whole of the design thoroughly in wax, making sure that the wax has penetrated. Wax both sides if necessary.

3   Remove the silk from the frame and scrunch it up in your hands so the wax cracks. If you added beeswax to your wax and it does not crack very well, pop it into the fridge for a little while. The wax will crack more effectively when it is fully chilled.

4   Thoroughly paint the cracked silk all over with a dark colour. The puffins were painted with black, as the birds themselves are quite bold. If the paint does not seem to be penetrating the cracks, brush quite hard and if necessary paint the back as well. Leave it to dry.

5   Remove the wax in the usual way, between sheets of newspaper using an iron. Finish as appropriate.

Finished puffins with the wax removed.

8 Experimental, Fun Techniques

HELIOGRAPHY

At first glance you are not quite aware of this technique, but on closer inspection it is really effective, yet subtle. The heliographic technique relies on sunshine, which in this country is not always forthcoming, but it can also be achieved with the use of a halogen lamp. For the best results use Setacolour transparent, which is a brand of fabric paint somewhat thicker than normal silk paints, and it will in fact paint on any fabric. For the following project mix one part Setacolour to two parts water. When new brands of dyes and paints come on to the market it is worth experimenting to see if they will produce the same effect.

Two scarves created using the heliographic technique.

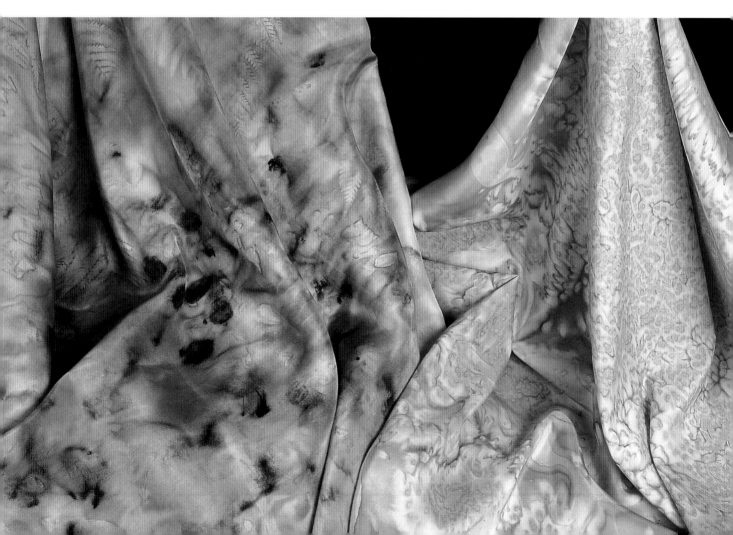

Marabou silk paints will give very good results, but for this project we will use Setacolour.

The effect of this technique is produced by a design of tools, flowers or leaves, for example, being placed on top of the wet painted silk and left out in the sun to dry. Once the silk has dried and the items lifted off, a lighter impression of the shape is left behind on the silk; it is as though the sun has bleached out the colour.

When I first experimented with this technique I hit several snags, so I will mention them. I had attached the silk to the frame in the usual way, and as I wanted to have a very loose interpretation of a hedgerow, I painted random bright colours: yellow for celandines and dandelions, pink for foxgloves, plus various greens for the grasses and blue for the sky. While it was quite wet I lay foxgloves and grasses on top of the painting and carefully took the screen out into the sunshine. The experiment failed miser-

ably. The silk was too thick and heavy, I had not wet the silk sufficiently and the foxgloves were too bulky and fleshy and created an indefinite shape. Generally, it was too ambitious for a first attempt. So I tried again, repainting and wetting the screen and laying ferns in the sky. Out again into the sun and this time it worked beautifully!

On another attempt I cut out plenty of fish shapes, laid them on to a blue/green painted silk and took it out carefully for the sun to do its work. However, the wind decided to blow and the fish fluttered away. Indoors once again I cut out more shapes, which I then wet so that they would stick to the wet silk. The lawn had just been mowed, so I scattered some cut daisies and salt over the wet screen. Out into the sun once again and the fish shapes stayed in place for quite a while, but as they dried out they began to curl. On facing the screen about an hour later, I was amazed as it was absolutely gorgeous! The fish having

Fern impression left after putting screen in the sun.

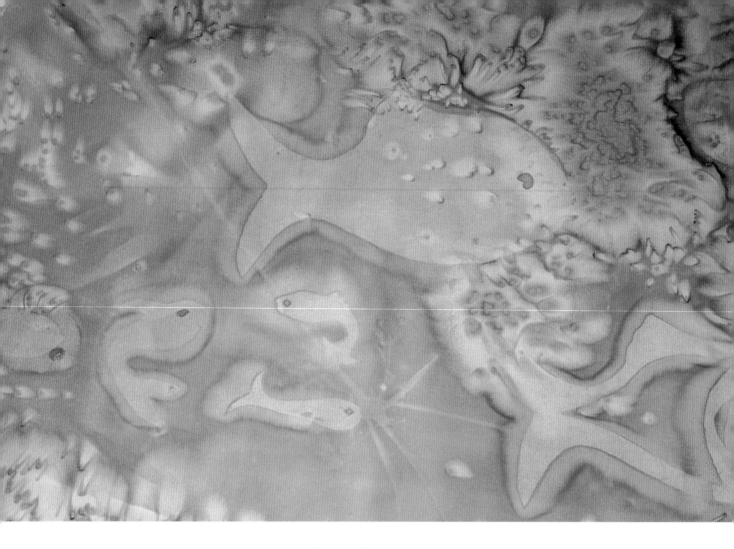

Detail of fabric – fish shapes were laid on to the silk with salt.

curled had left an effect on the silk which made it look as if they were actually swimming, whilst in amongst the salt effect were the most perfect daisies.

Flowers

This project is based on the above experience.

EQUIPMENT

- silk

- frame

- masking tape and silk pins

- brushes (sizes 6 and 8) and large brush

- Setacolour transparent (or Marabou silk paints)

- water pot

- plate or palette for mixing colours

- paper towel

- flowers and leaves to lay on the silk

- coarse sea salt

- halogen lamp, or better still a bright sunny day

INSTRUCTIONS

1   Cover and prepare the frame with masking tape and silk.

2   Quickly paint large areas of colour over your silk.

3   Lay on your flowers and leaves. Try to make sure they lay flat. If using a dandelion leaf, for example, I would suggest that you run it under the tap before laying it on the silk. The extra water will help it to stay in place. If necessary, put heavier items on top to anchor things down. Choose different objects to lay on the silk, such as household items, shells, pasta shapes, doilies, or experiment with a variety of paper shapes.

4   Scatter some coarse sea salt into the spaces.

5   Carefully take the screen outside and leave in the sun to dry. If you are using a halogen lamp, make sure it is directly overhead so that the whole area has the same intensity of light. The lamp should be about 16in away from the silk.

6   When it is dry, remove the flowers and leaves.

7   Although the sun has dried and fixed the colour, it would be wise to fix it again using the appropriate technique.

SILK VELVET

The luxury and softness of velvet is out of this world, although I have come across one or two people who simply cannot bear to touch it. Devore silk is once again in vogue, but it is expensive and much sought after, so why not produce your own designs. Having found the magic solution in the form of Fiberetch, it is now within everyone's capability, although I would recommend experimenting on small pieces of silk before tackling a large project. The solution has to be used with great care and you must follow the instructions to the

Setacolour transparent used to produce heliographic effect.

Materials for devore.

letter. Fiber-etch is useful for all sorts of techniques, but in this instance we are interested in its use with velvet. Plain, natural-coloured velvet is best if you wish to paint, stencil or spray your designs and colours. If you are just wanting to produce devore, coloured silk velvet is ideal.

The name of the product suggests how it works. The velvet is etched with chemicals, 'burning' away the pile but leaving the ground fabric intact. Use this solution in a well-ventilated place, as it does have a strong, pungent smell, and wear protective gloves at all times throughout the process. Having experimented I found the best method was to apply the solution carefully to the reverse side of the velvet. Drawing with the bottle directly on to the silk can produce blobs, which is an excessive amount and can burn through the ground fabric when it is heated. For line drawing I found it ideal, but you do need practice. For more detailed designs I suggest using a sponge; a doily, for instance, produces a lovely effect.

Once the solution has been applied, let it dry naturally, or better still use a hairdryer. When it is dry, iron the pile side of the velvet with the iron on a wool setting. The pile will gradually look charred. Take great care at this stage, as it can easily burn straight through and you will be left with holes. Keep stopping to check the progress and as soon as the pile starts to crumble the job is complete. Wash it thoroughly once it is finished, and tumble dry to bring the pile back. Velvet looks wonderful when painted – the dyes always appear bright and rich. I prefer to use steam-fixed dyes as the iron-fixed paints clog up the pile, but procion dyes are also excellent on velvet.

PENS AND CRAYONS

Fabric pens are markers, ideal for creating surface decoration and for use as

(a)

(d)

(a) Etched swirls painted with steam-fixed inks.

(b) Doily design etched on to silk velvet.

(c) Daisy flowers drawn using Fiber-etch.

(d) Random drawn shapes using Fiber-etch to produce devore.

(e) Fleur-de-lis design stamped on to silk velvet.

(f) Stencilled velvet.

(b)

(e)

(c)

(f)

highlighters. Permanent markers can also be used on silk. Some are refillable, and all are usually available at good craft shops. There is a wide selection of brands to choose from, but I would suggest trying a variety of different nib sizes to find which suits you best. These pens are also ideal for children, as they are so easy to use and are non-toxic. The lines do not bleed unless water is added, in which case they prove to be quite versatile. Pens and outliners come in all forms: glitter, pearlized, metallic and fluorescent, and they can be used on dark-coloured backgrounds.

Do be open-minded about them. The market now has so many to offer that it would be a good idea to build up a sample book, showing various examples used on a variety of silks to note how the pens react: do they spread, mix, spread

Design using fabric pens.

Design using outliners.

with water, or react with salt? All this information will prove useful at a later date and provide a wealth of ideas.

Fabric crayons are available as steam-fixed or iron-fixed. Some crayons can be used directly on to silk and melt with the heat from a hairdryer or iron. Steam-fixed crayons can be used as a resist to dyes once they have been melted; the iron-fixed crayons do not resist.

You could also use transfer crayons, which act as their name implies. Once drawn on to a sheet of paper, they will

Design using steam-fixed crayons with dye painted inside.

Rubbings can be made with fabric crayons to good effect.

Transfer crayons.

Outliners in a range
of colours.

OVENS AND MICROWAVES

A strange idea to associate with silk painting, but there are several brands of dye that are ideal to use in the microwave and oven. I suggest you ask your stockist what their brands are capable of achieving and how they can be used. Over the years of silk painting I have tried some bizarre techniques, but you do need to check things out, especially if you are a complete beginner. One of the latest techniques is to use Silk Art, a steam-fixed ink which can be used in the microwave. The smell can be quite overpowering, so use it in a well-ventilated area. This is a super technique to use when in a group, as the range of colours mixed by members will be out of this world. It produces a superb blended effect and, of course, all projects are fixed at the same time.

transfer on to silk when ironed. You must remember that the image will be reversed, especially when using letters and numbers.

Puffpaint is available in tubes in a range of colours. Once heat is applied to a line it 'puffs out'. This is quite interesting to use, although it is not always successful on silk.

Puffpaint on silk.

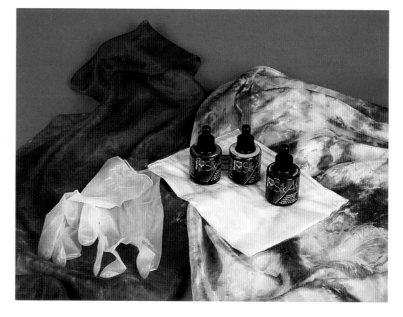

Materials for
microwaving scarves.

(opposite) Scarves produced with the help of a microwave.

EQUIPMENT

- silk

- Marabou Silk Art

- household vinegar

- rubber gloves (essential)

- newspaper or plastic sheet

- microwave pot with a hole in the lid

- microwave (600w power)

INSTRUCTIONS

1   Soak the untreated silk in vinegar, wring it out and drape it on to the plastic sheet. For a different effect you can leave it crumpled in the sink.

2   Drop or brush the ink on to the silk.

3   Put the silk in the microwave pot, cover with the lid and then place it in the microwave for four minutes at full power. Use a well-ventilated area.

4   When it has finished, let the silk cool a little. Wash it in warm soapy water, then rinse and iron it.

The next example uses a conventional oven, iron-fixed paints and produces a bark-like texture.

As you follow this technique you may be alarmed at the burnt state of the silk once it has been 'cooked', but do not worry as it will be fine once washed.

Silk wound around a terracotta pot prior to placing in the oven.

Scarf with batik effect produced by baking.

EQUIPMENT

- silk, preferably a long rectangular piece rather than a square as it has to be twisted

- medium terracotta flower pot, 3–4in diameter at the top

- iron-fixed paints

- large brush

- water pot

- plastic sheet

- rubber gloves (essential)

- plate or palette to mix colours

- oven

INSTRUCTIONS

1   Put the scarf on to the plastic sheet and paint it thoroughly with colour. Do not water the colour down too much, and for the best results use the paint neat.

2   Twist the scarf very tightly and wind it around the flower pot. Leave it to dry. This is best prepared either first thing in the morning or last thing at night so that it has a long time to dry.

3   Put the oven on and when it has reached 120°C/250°F/gas mark 1, put the flower pot in and leave it for twenty minutes.

4   Be careful as you take the pot out as it will be very hot. Leave it to cool.

5   Carefully unwind the silk, which will look as though it has been burnt. You might think it will crack and tear as it is untwisted, but it will be fine.

6   Wash the silk in warm soapy water, rinse and iron it.

9 Fixing

There are three ways of fixing your work, depending on which dyes you have used. Always check the fixing instructions when buying dyes, as they do vary and you will be so frustrated if, when you have completed a painting, you do not have the correct equipment.

IRON-FIXING

This is the easiest method of fixing and is ideal for the beginner. Once your painting is finished and completely dry, iron it on the reverse side with a hot dry iron for two to three minutes. If you have used a hairdryer during painting you may well have fixed the colour, but always fix it again to be sure.

In some instances, coloured and metallic gutta can print on to the ironing board, so do be aware of this, as by the same method the print may iron back on to another piece of work. In the early days my board was covered in herons and ducks of all varieties.

LIQUID-FIXING

Some dyes are fixed using a liquid-fixer, which is painted over the dry finished painting. You need to check individual instructions, but the fixer is usually left on for about an hour before being rinsed in warm water. I have only used liquid-fixing on a few occasions, and it did make water-based gutta slightly sticky so take extra care.

STEAM-FIXING

Do make sure all surfaces are dry before getting out items for steaming, as the work will be vulnerable to water until after it has been fixed. Steam-fixed dyes do produce the most vibrant of colours and you do not have to have expensive equipment in order to finish your work. A pressure cooker is useful for small pieces.

Lay your work flat on a piece of paper (lining paper is ideal) and roll the silk and paper together. Curl the roll to fit into the pressure cooker, leaving a space

Pressure cooker with silk to be rolled ready for steaming.

around the edge. Before putting it in, wrap the parcel well in tinfoil. No water must get into your package as it can ruin a piece of work, so careful attention at this stage will save any heartache later. Put the parcel on top of an upturned pudding basin inside the pressure cooker. To make extra sure water and condensation will not get in, cut a foil circle and lay it over the top of the parcel so any water can drip straight into the bottom of the pressure cooker. Add about 1–1½in of water to the cooker, seal the lid and steam for approximately 30–45 minutes. When it is finished, carefully remove and allow the parcel to cool a little.

TIP:

• Do not reuse the tinfoil, as once it has been used it starts to break down and tiny holes occur which could allow water to get in and damage your work.

As I mentioned earlier, water-based gutta will become sticky during the steaming process, so make sure the work is wrapped in sufficient paper. As an alternative to a pressure cooker you can use a steamer over a saucepan which will be equally successful. Follow the same method for making the parcel, but you will need to steam for approximately two hours. Do keep checking that you have sufficient water in the saucepan at all times.

Large Steamers

If you are tackling large lengths of silk it would be worth sending them away for fixing, as some silk suppliers offer a steaming service. Large steamers are available; vertical steamers are particularly expensive, but will steam widths up to one-and-a-half metres and lengths of up to fifty metres depending on the thickness of the silk. For the beginner this will be quite unnecessary, but a long steamer,

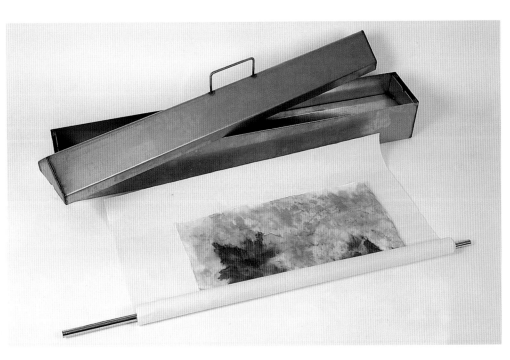

Long steamer to fit over two rings of a cooker.

which will fit over two rings on your cooker, could be considered if you are tackling many scarves or large paintings.

This steamer has proved extremely useful, taking approximately one hour to steam six scarves, increasing the length of steaming for the relative extra quantity of work. The water level must be checked to ensure it never dries out.

WASHING

After fixing, wash your work in warm soapy water, using a liquid such as Stergene. Once it has been washed, rinse it in warm water to which a few drops of vinegar have been added; this helps to bring out the sheen of the silk. Roll the silk in a towel to remove the excess water, then iron whilst damp on the reverse side.

If a water-based gutta has been used, it should all have washed out; wash again if it has not. If the spirit-based gutta has not washed out, soak the silk in white spirit for a few minutes, and when it has

turned sticky and jelly-like it can be carefully removed. Another wash will be necessary in this case. Metallic gutta needs to be ironed prior to washing after having been steamed.

REMOVING WAX

This is a tedious process and uses a large amount of newspaper quite quickly. Put two or three layers of paper on top of the batik, with a dozen or so sheets underneath, then iron. The wax will melt so quickly that you will need to replace all the paper for subsequent repeats of the process. Continue until all the wax has been removed. For batik, although you have ironed to remove the wax, you will still need to steam if you used steam-fixed dyes. After fixing for either method, the silk may still feel stiff. To remove the stiffness, immerse the silk in a bowl with some white spirit. Leave it for about five minutes and hang it out to dry. Wash it once more in the usual way, dry and then iron it.

10 Design Tips

MISTAKES

All silk painters make mistakes at some point. When a bleed occurs it can be very frustrating; they are often difficult to hide, so adapt them as part of the design, perhaps as an extra leaf or petal. If the colour has seeped into the background then add more of that colour to the background and it will look

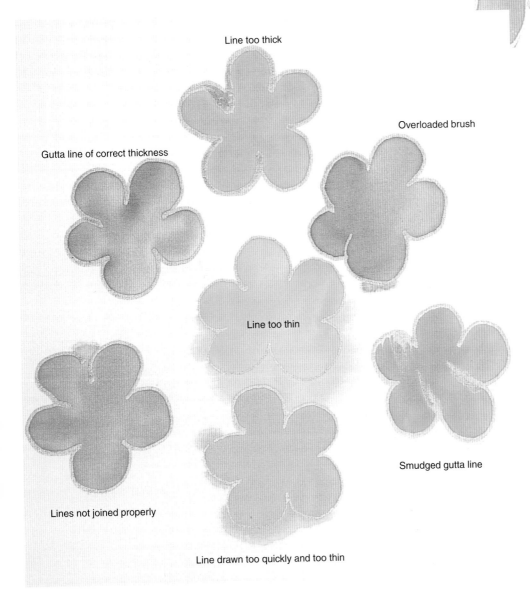

Line too thick

Overloaded brush

Gutta line of correct thickness

Line too thin

Smudged gutta line

Lines not joined properly

Line drawn too quickly and too thin

intentional. Repair broken gutta lines once the colour has dried, but do not use a hairdryer to do this as you will fix the colour if you have used paints. Make sure the gutta has dried before continuing.

'LEFTOVERS'

What can you do with your odd bits of silk, especially as there will be plenty of them? Making cards of all shapes and sizes is often the most successful use, smaller pieces being ideal for gift tags. Often our leftover pieces or 'mistakes'

will have interesting paint effects which can be isolated and highlighted in a card. Small pieces of silk are also ideal for brooches and earrings.

Greetings Cards

Cut the card yourself to make greetings cards, or save time and much frustration and choose from the many that are available, precut and ready to use. To attach the silk to the card use double-sided tape on two sides of the aperture only. Do not use glue as this will seep through and ruin the finish, and in time it will

Screen of part-painted silk for greetings cards.

Made-up cards.

Blank card, scissors,
double-sided tape and silk.

become discoloured. I have tried a solid glue stick, and when used sparingly it can be helpful.

I have made thousands of cards over the years, so I know how easy they are to do. The secret is not to try too hard or fiddle too much with the silk, pulling it in all directions. I tend to use three-fold cards as they have a neat finish, but two-fold cards can be just as effective.

First attach double-sided tape to the two longer sides of the aperture, lay in the silk, which has been trimmed to overlap the aperture by ¼in (5mm); this will also be halfway across the tape. Hold the silk down on the right hand side and carefully peel off the top of the tape under the silk. Tap the silk down just sufficient to secure it. There should be no need to peel off the silk to reposition it as this leads to distortion and it will not flatten again. With one side fixed, carefully peel off the tape from the other side of the aperture. A swift swipe across the silk from the fixed side to the opposite side will be sufficient to anchor it to the tape. Silk is so light that it will not be necessary to put tape on all four sides. If you have used a three-fold card, then fold over the third side to cover the silk. The tape left uncovered by the silk will be sufficient to hold the cover over the silk.

Jewellery

Jewellery findings are available at good craft outlets and are very easy to make up.

BROOCH

Lay your piece of silk flat and draw round your shape on to the silk. Cut with a ¼in (5mm) allowance from the line, as this will be needed to wrap under the shape. Cover both sides of the shape with double-sided tape. Attach the silk to the top surface and press it round the shape to stick to the reverse side. It is advisable to put a little glue around the edge in this instance to attach the shape to the wooden frame, taking care that the glue does not seep out. Glue the clip to the back of the brooch with strong glue. Some findings have little metal clips to hold the silk in, so it would be best to use jewellers' pliers to fix the silk in properly.

FRAMING

Try padding your silk prior to mounting and framing. When it is padded the light has a better chance of catching the sheen of the silk and highlighting areas of the design. If you do not use padding, mount your work over white card, as the white will highlight the colours to produce a really bright effect. It is worth taking your work to a professional framer as they often suggest a mount and moulding which really does justice to the work.

DESIGN SOURCES

I often hear people say: 'I shall never be able to do silk painting. I can't draw, let alone design.' This is nonsense! Anyone can do silk painting: my youngest pupil was six and the eldest 84 years old. It has been a privilege to tutor so many people over the years, each and every one bringing something special to the work. Designs and inspiration are all around us; it is just that most of us are occupied with daily jobs and forget how to play. We feel that we have to have a finished, perfect piece by the end of the day and overlook the fun to be had along the way.

What you design really depends on the mood you are in, the time available and your immediate circumstances. If

Jewellery findings.

you are working with a group of people, you may well have chosen a theme or colour range to work within. Write down all the things that come to mind relating to that project. Start a source book: cut out articles and pictures, or even words that might inspire you, but gradually build up a record of ideas. Also, test your colours on a variety of silks. You can then refer back to the various results and try to recreate them.

Rubbings are another great source of inspiration, as is anything that has a surface texture, for example bark, leaves or stonework. There is bound to be a technique covered in this book that will help you to achieve the texture that you are after.

Designs do not have to be 'true to life', they may be merely shapes that make an interesting pattern. Colour can create a mood and you may wish to collect

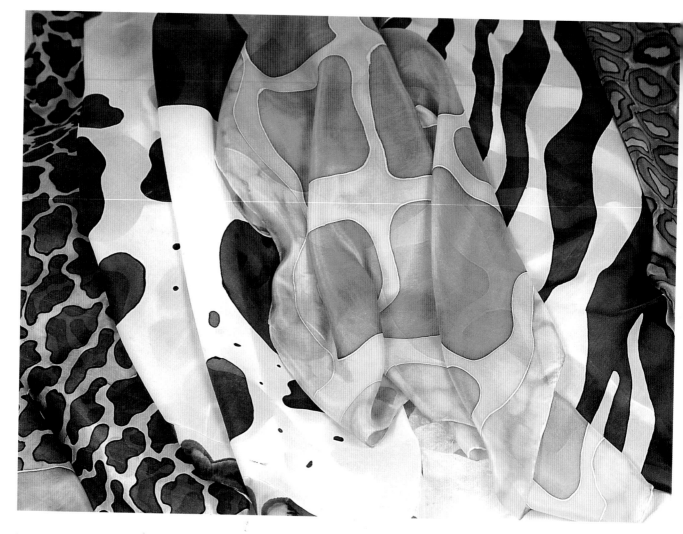

Scarves with animal fur print designs.

landscapes or skies. How often have we seen the sun setting and said: 'No-one would believe the colour of that sky.'

To start you off, I have painted a few scarves based on animal fur prints.

The designs were taken from a variety of photos and illustrations. The line drawings may be useful to you.

If you have a camera, try to keep it with you and it will be surprising how often you will want to use it. Make a folder or scrap book of ideas, so that when you next want to do a silk painting or make a card for a friend, you will always have inspiration nearby.

Printed Gutta

A number of techniques have been covered in this book, the combinations of which are endless, but some of you may still need to overcome the feeling that you cannot draw. Arty's, a silk painting supplier based in Surrey, have come to your aid. They have a magnificent catalogue and supply of ready-printed items, so all you need to do is paint. Purists will throw their hands up in despair, but that is fine. I believe that once a painter's confidence has been built they will wish to experiment and create their own

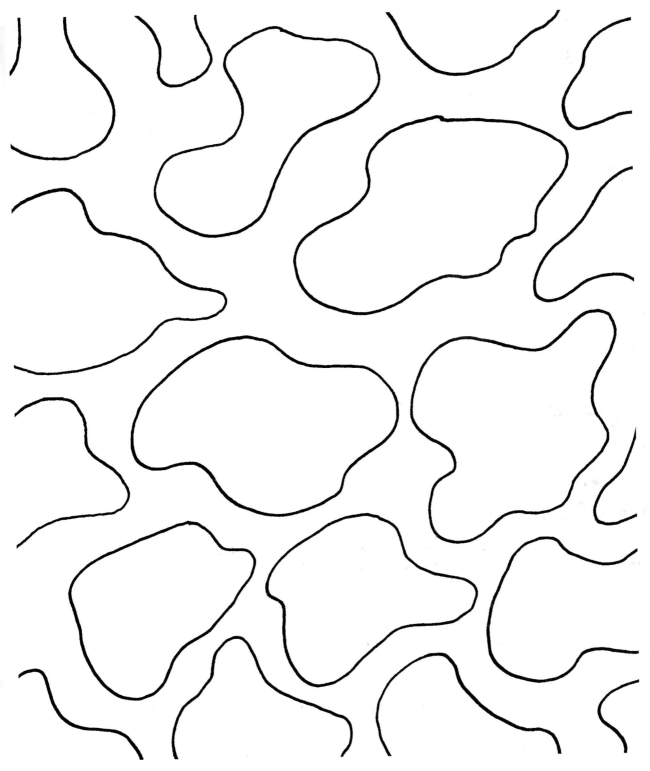

Cheetah line drawing.

Zebra line drawing.

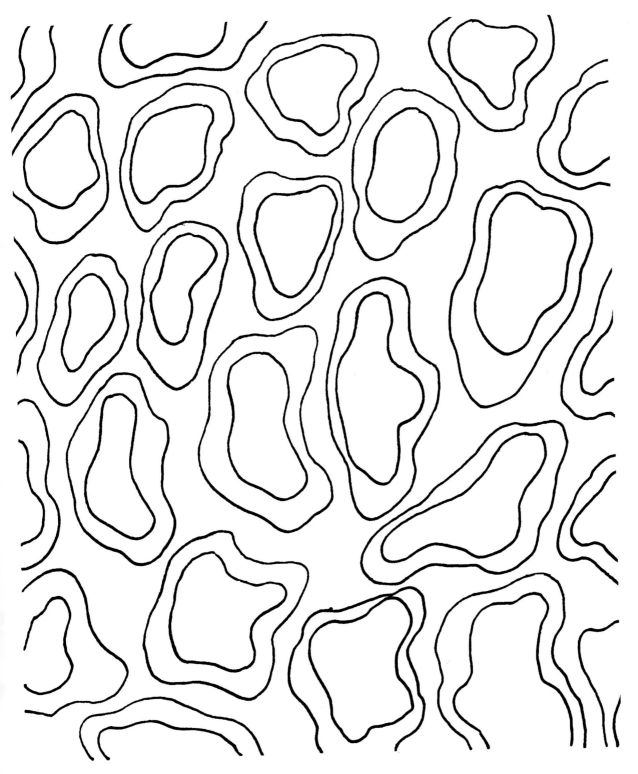

Leopard line drawing.

Vegetation – a printed gutta
scarf.

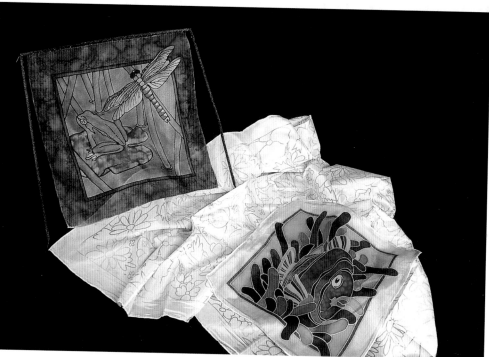

Printed gutta hankies.

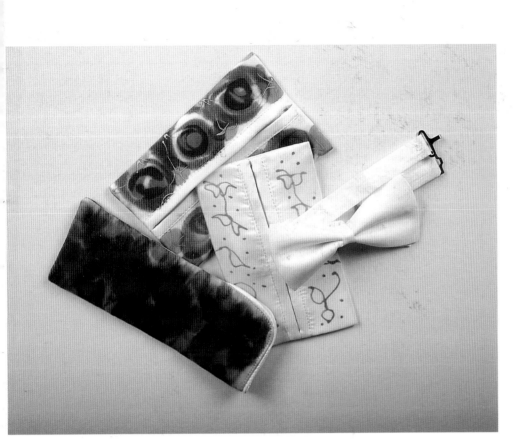

Tissue holder, spectacles case and bow tie – made-up silk items ready to paint.

Tie and mobile by Nik Jory.

designs. If these printed gutta items start people painting and attempting this fascinating craft, then so be it; everyone has to start somewhere. The selection of designs and items to paint is extensive, so have fun using colour!

It is amazing how, and in what context, silk can be used. This book has been written to inspire the beginner and get you started on a craft that can quite simply take over your life.

Arty's stock a wealth of wonderful silk, from plain to jacquard design, silk by the metre and ready-rolled scarves in an amazing selection of sizes. It also has a selection of ready made-up items just waiting to be painted, including smaller items which can be a fiddle to make, but which would make ideal gifts. The pleasure then is in the painting.

Nik Jory's fish mobile glows perfectly, especially when hung near a window, but preferably with no direct sun as this will eventually alter the colour, however well it has been fixed. Silk paintings, like any other form of painting, watercolours in particular, will deteriorate if they are hung in direct sunlight.

Glossary

Anti-spread/Antifusant – a clear or milky liquid which when painted on to silk dries to form a barrier, which in turn stops the spread of the paints and dyes.

Autofade Pen – a pen which can be used instead of a soft pencil. The colour fades within a few hours or as soon as water is applied.

Batik – the process of applying molten wax to fabric to produce intricate designs.

Devore – the technique of etching patterns on to silk velvet.

Diffusing Medium/Diluant/Alcohol – a thinner which can be added to paints to help them spread more evenly.

Fixing – setting the colour in the silk, leaving it ready to wash or dry clean where necessary.

Frame – a wooden structure to which the silk is pinned so it can sit proud of a flat surface, enabling various techniques of silk painting to be carried out.

Gutta – a resist which stops colours blending into one another. Available in tubes or bottles.

Gutta Bottle – a plastic bottle to which a gutta nib can be attached. It is then used as a gutta applicator.

Gutta Nib – a small metal nib which attaches to a gutta bottle to enable fine gutta lines to be drawn. The nibs are available with different sized nozzles.

Heliography – a method of printing/painting on silk using the sun or a halogen lamp.

Malmittel – a blender used in conjunction with silk paints instead of water to obtain and retain the subtlety of pastel shades.

Masking Tape – used to keep the frame clean and free of dye. Also used to anchor the silk to the frame.

Momme – a Chinese measurement for the weight of silk fabric per square metre. The unit 'momme' is equal to 4.306 grams per square metre.

Monoprint – a technique used to produce one-off printed designs.

Outliner – a resist available in metallic, pearlized and plain colours. When ironed it remains in the silk after washing.

Procion dyes – reactive cold water dyes.

Salt – used to produce random patterns when scattered on to wet painted silk. Different salts give different results.

Saturated Salt Solution – when painted on to silk and dried this solution produces a speckled quality when the silk is subsequently painted with dyes.

Silk – a wide variety of silk is available of varying weight and quality.

Silk Dyes – dyes fixed by steaming, producing vibrant colours.

Silk Paints – paints fixed by ironing; ideal for the beginner.

Silk Pins – three-pointed silk pins used to attach silk to a frame. They are very sharp so will not snag the silk if inserted properly.

Slub – an unregular, small lump which occurs in the thread taken from the cocoon, which is incorporated into the silk fabric.

Stenter Pins – ideal for silk with rolled edges or silk velvet, as they keep the silk away from the frame. They have prongs which are bent at right angles to hook into the velvet, and attach to the frame with rubber bands.

Template – a shape around which you draw on to the silk.

Thickener (*Epaissisant*) – a thick, clear substance which can be mixed with dyes to prevent them spreading on silk, and which enables a variety of techniques such as stencilling and printing to be used.

Tjanting – a tool used in batik that has a copper bowl to contain wax and a spout to enable fine lines to be drawn.

Wax – used as a resist in batik. Paraffin wax is ideal for the cracking technique, whilst beeswax is ideal for fine detail work.

Suppliers

Great Britain

Wide selection of silk supplies:
George Weil & Son Limited
Reading Arch Road
Redhill
Surrey RH1 1HG
01737 778868

Amazing selection of silk fabrics and items:
Arty's
Reading Arch Road
Redhill
Surrey RH1 1HG
01737 778868

Marabou silk paints:
Edding UK Limited
Merlin Centre
Acrewood Way
St. Albans
Hertfordshire AL4 0JY
01727 846688

Silk importers:
Pongees
28–30 Moxton Square
London N1 6NN
0171 739 9130

Silk scarves:
Pure Silk (Eddie Salter)
Old Church Room
Hill Row
Haddenham
Cambridge CB6 3TQ

Silk, paints and accessories:
Ad Infinitum
Foundry Court
Wadebridge
Cornwall PL7 7QN
01208 815887

Silk:
Whaley's (Bradford) Limited
Harris Court
Bradford
West Yorkshire BD7 4EQ
01274 576718

Card blanks and findings for jewellery:
Impress
Slough Farm
Westhall
Halesworth
Suffolk IP19 8RN
0198 678 1422

Silk Painting Suppliers Abroad

Belgium:
La Fourmi
Rue Vanderkinder 236
1180 Brussels

France:
Ponsard Freres
28, Rue du Sentier
75002 Paris

Germany:
Galerie Smend
Mainzer Straße 31
Postfach 250360
5000 Köln

USA:
Dharma Trading Co.
PO Box 150916
San Rafael
California 94915

Ivy Imports
5410 Annapolis Road
Bladensburg
Maryland 20710

The Embroidery Guild of America
200 Fourth Avenue
Louiseville
Kentucky 40202

Australia:
Oetero Pty
PO Box 324
Coogee
New South Wales 2034

Raw Silk
183 Grange Road
PO Box 255
Findon
SA 5023

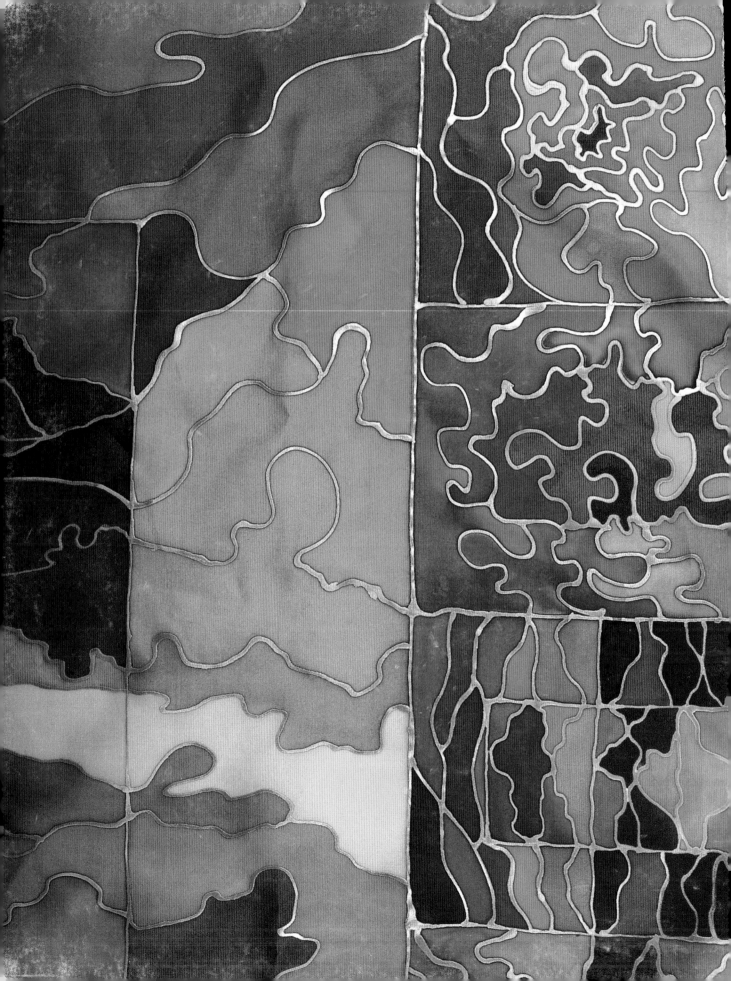

Index